Preparation for Writing Practice

To help your child learn to write effectively, we recommend the following pre

T0115750

1. Development of Postural Control

- It is important for your child to be able to keep their body balanced while ng their hands to stabilize).
- When writing, ensure your child's back is straight, elbows and knees are bent at 90-degree angles, feet are flat on the floor or on the chair's footrest, and the paper or workbook is angled with the corner of the page pointing toward the child's torso.
- If you notice your child consistently sitting with poor posture—leaning on one arm or slouching—this is not a sign of laziness or a lack of motivation.
- Try incorporating one of these core exercises into your child's daily routine to help strengthen their postural chain: ride a bike, swim, jump, climb, crab-walk, do sit-ups, roll from their back to their belly in both directions, dance, swing, bounce on a trampoline, or play Red Light, Green Light.

2. Development of Tripod Grasp and Fine Motor Skills

- To hold a pencil, children need to practice grabbing and pinching objects daily to strengthen the small muscles in their hands and wrists.
- Let them experience a wide range of activities to build these muscles, such as playing with building blocks, clay, puzzles, or origami.
- Research shows that if we engage fine motor muscles in a multisensory way, kids will develop writing skills much earlier and will have more fun while writing! Try the following activities: drawing in salt, dirt, cinnamon, sand, flour; picking up pom-poms with tweezers; using a hole punch; taking stickers off a sticker sheet and sticking them on a piece of paper; and playing with clothespins.
- If you don't have enough time to practice with your child, you can incorporate fine motor activities into your daily routine, such as allowing your child to pick up and put cereal in their own mouth or helping them learn to pick up and put blocks away when it is time to clean up.

3. Keep It Fun

- Make writing feel like play! For example, while using this book, you could ask your child to pretend that the pencil tip is a race car that cannot go off the dotted-line track—otherwise, it will crash.
- If your child starts to scribble or do something silly, this is a sign that they are feeling uncomfortable or nervous about proceeding. Give some gentle encouragement and ask them if they would like a blank sheet of paper to make a drawing instead. Scribbling is just as important to writing development as letter tracing.
- Remember, writing is HARD. Many different systems of the brain and body must work together for children to learn to write properly. Children need visual perception, visual memory, spatial awareness, sensory processing, executive functioning skills, and self-regulation, as well as fine motor skills, bilateral coordination between both sides of the body, and a strong core and attention span to be successful writers.

Happy writing!

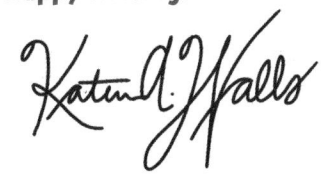

Katerina A. Walls, Cognitive Development Specialist

Basic Lines Practice drawing basic lines. Trace the lines from ●→ to ●.

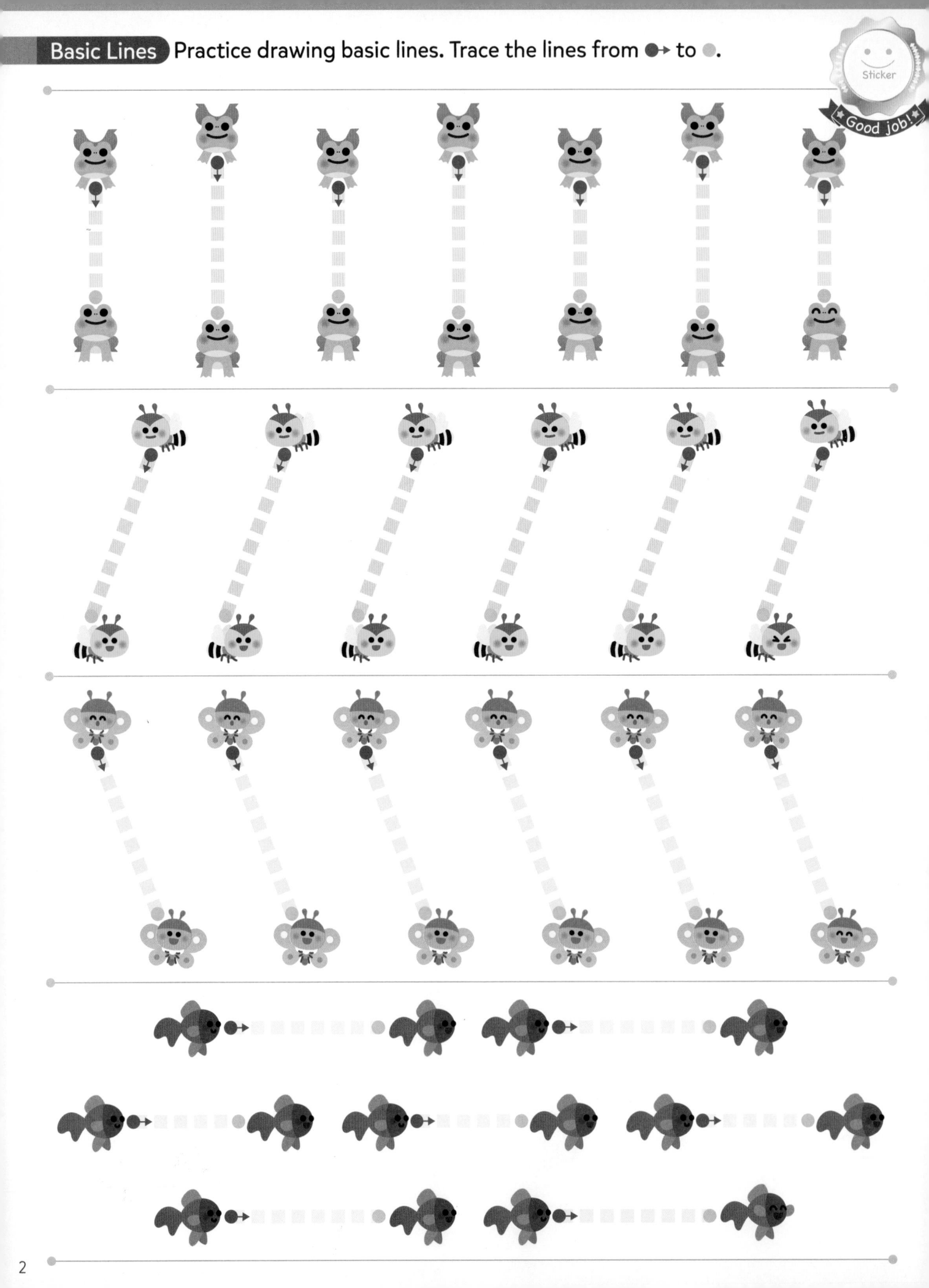

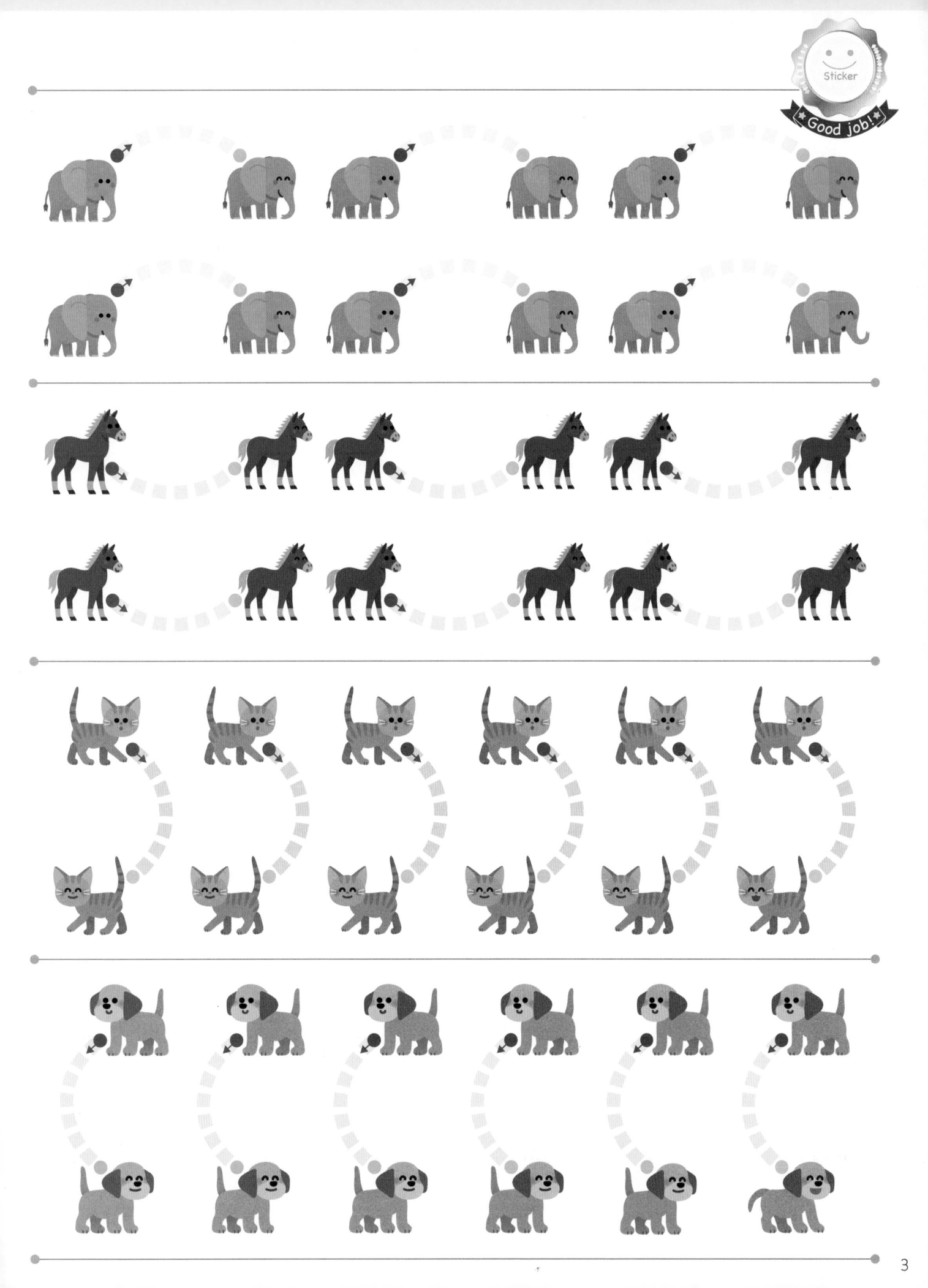
Sticker
Good job!

Trace the lines from ●→ to ●.

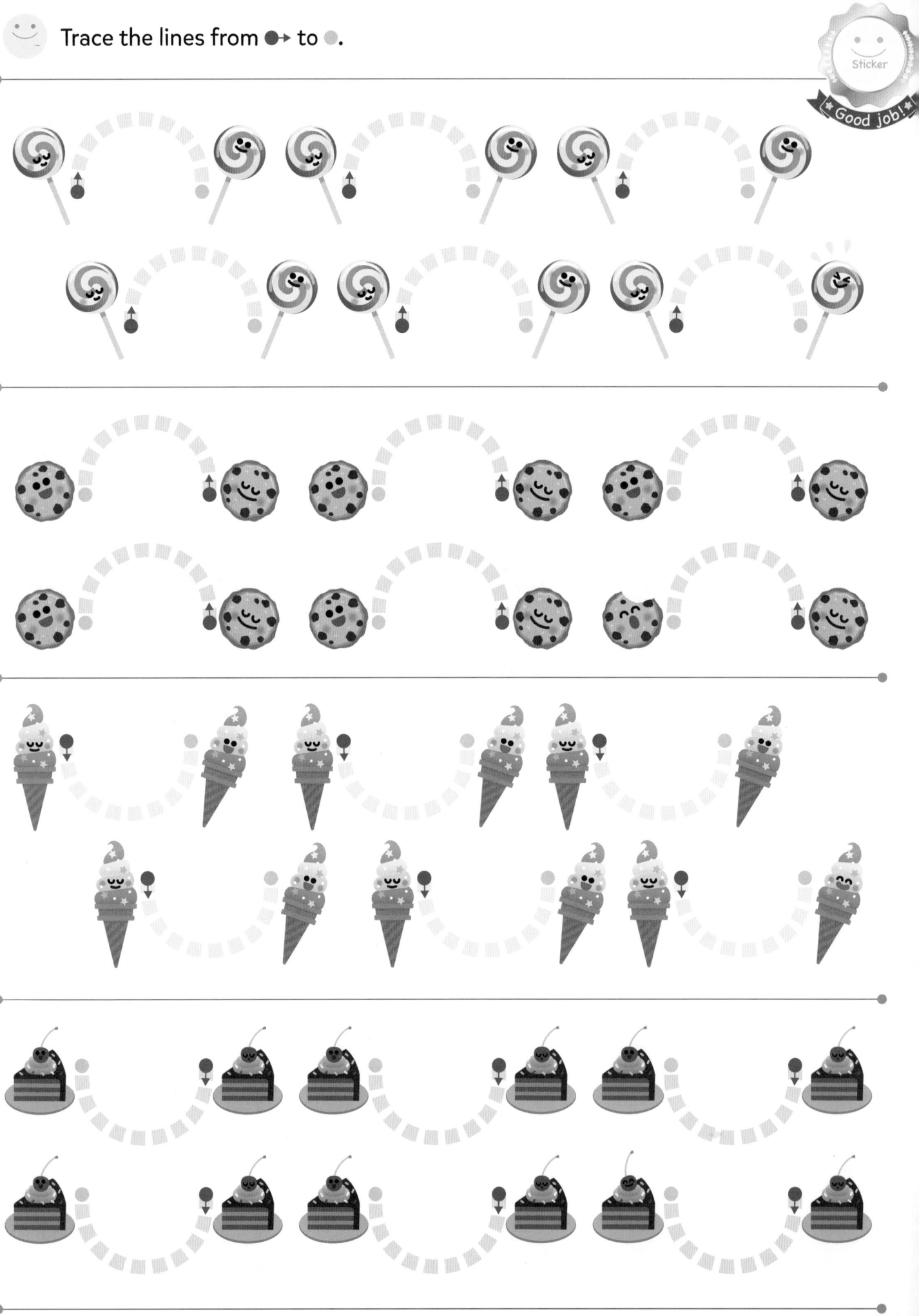

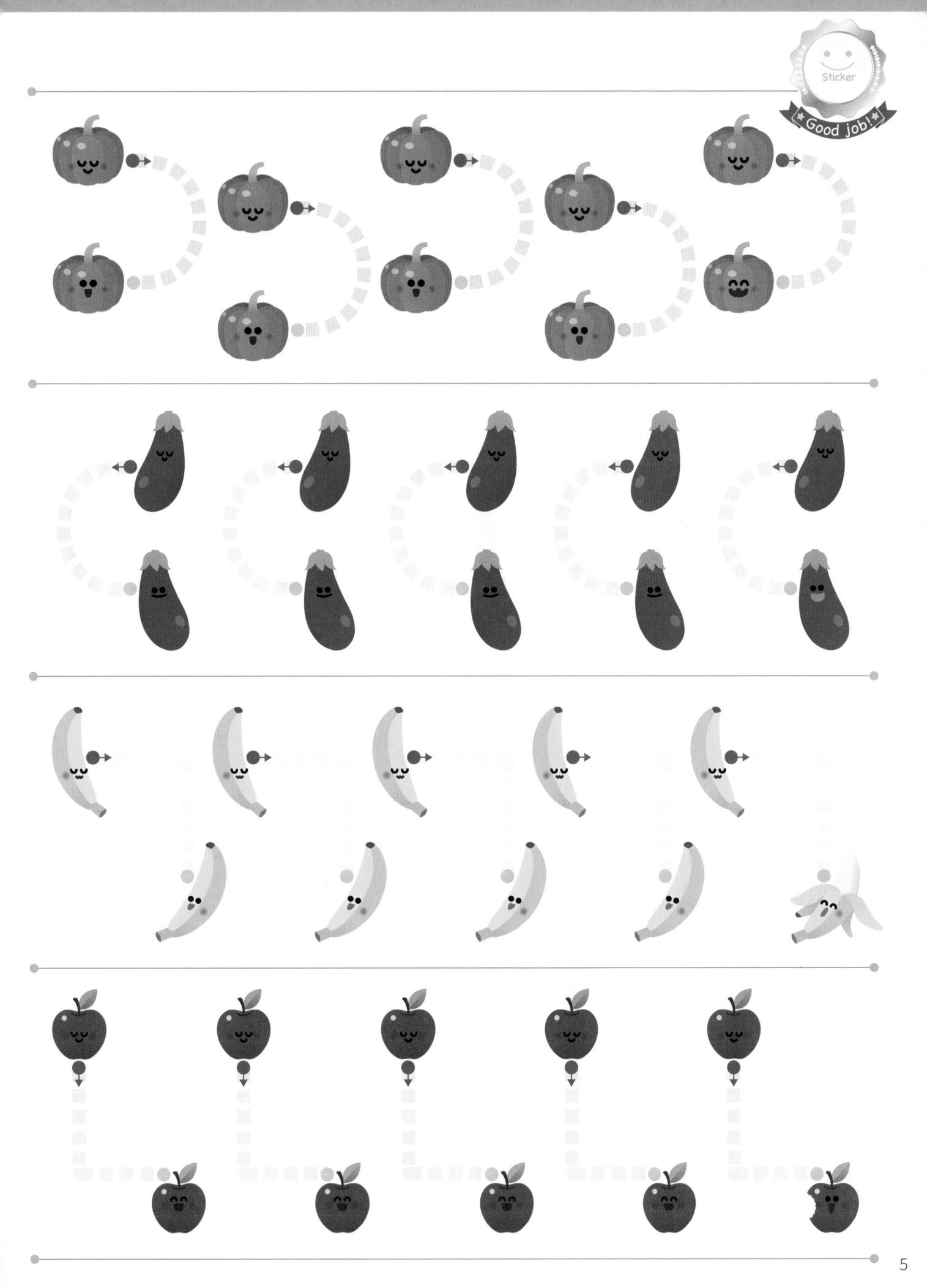
Sticker
Good job!

Trace the lines from ●→ to ●.

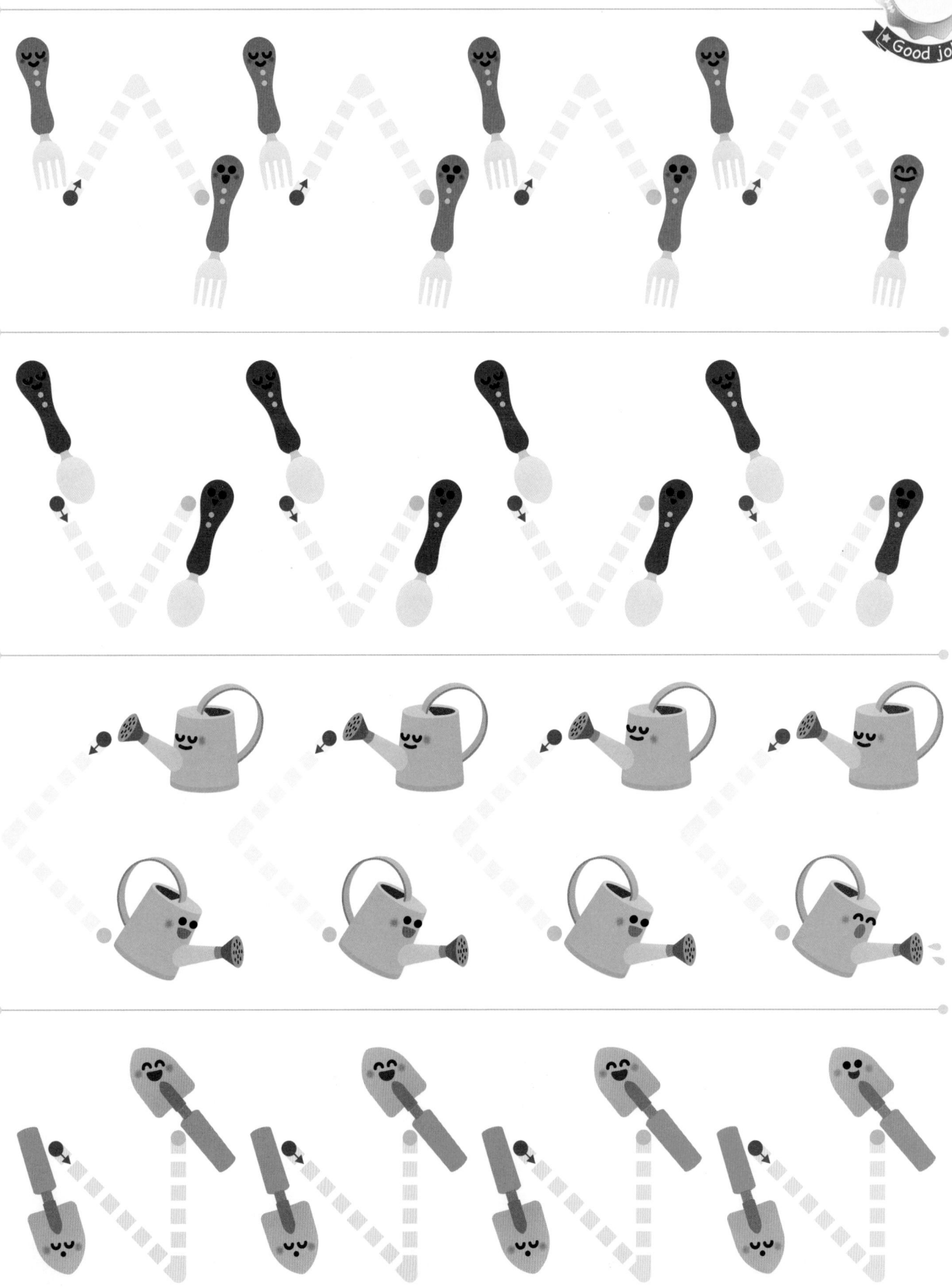

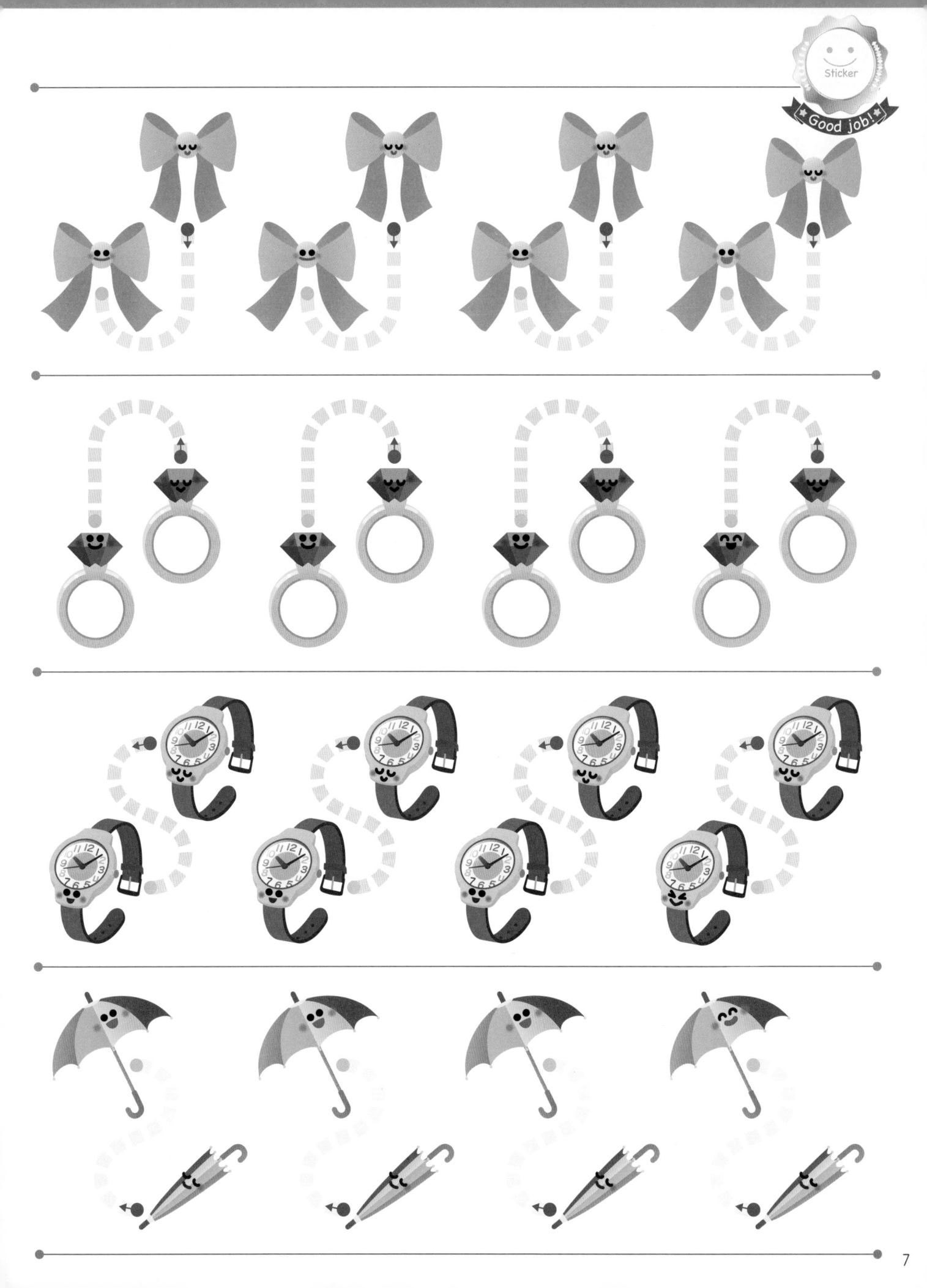
Sticker
Good job!

Trace the lines from ●→ to ●.

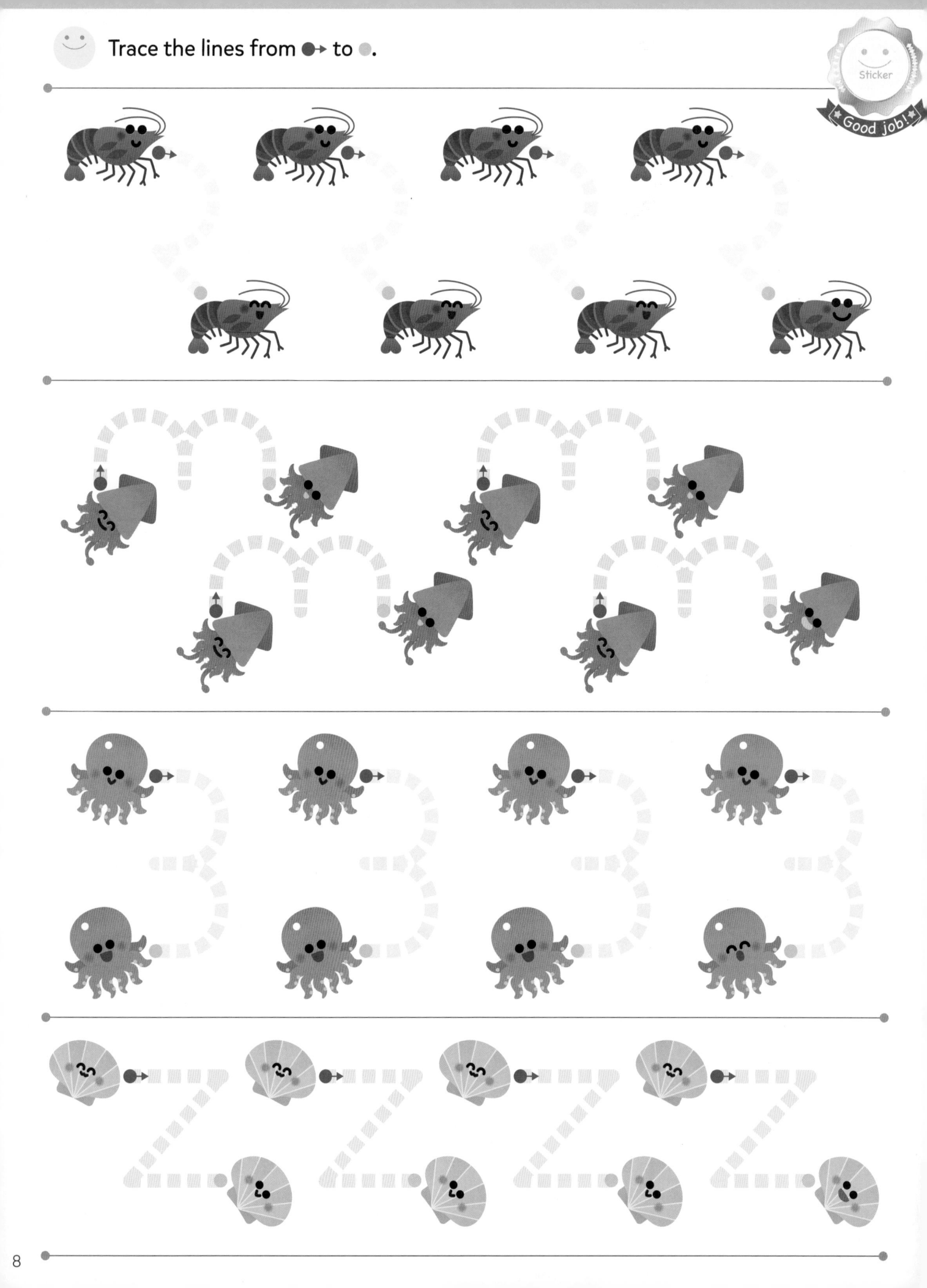

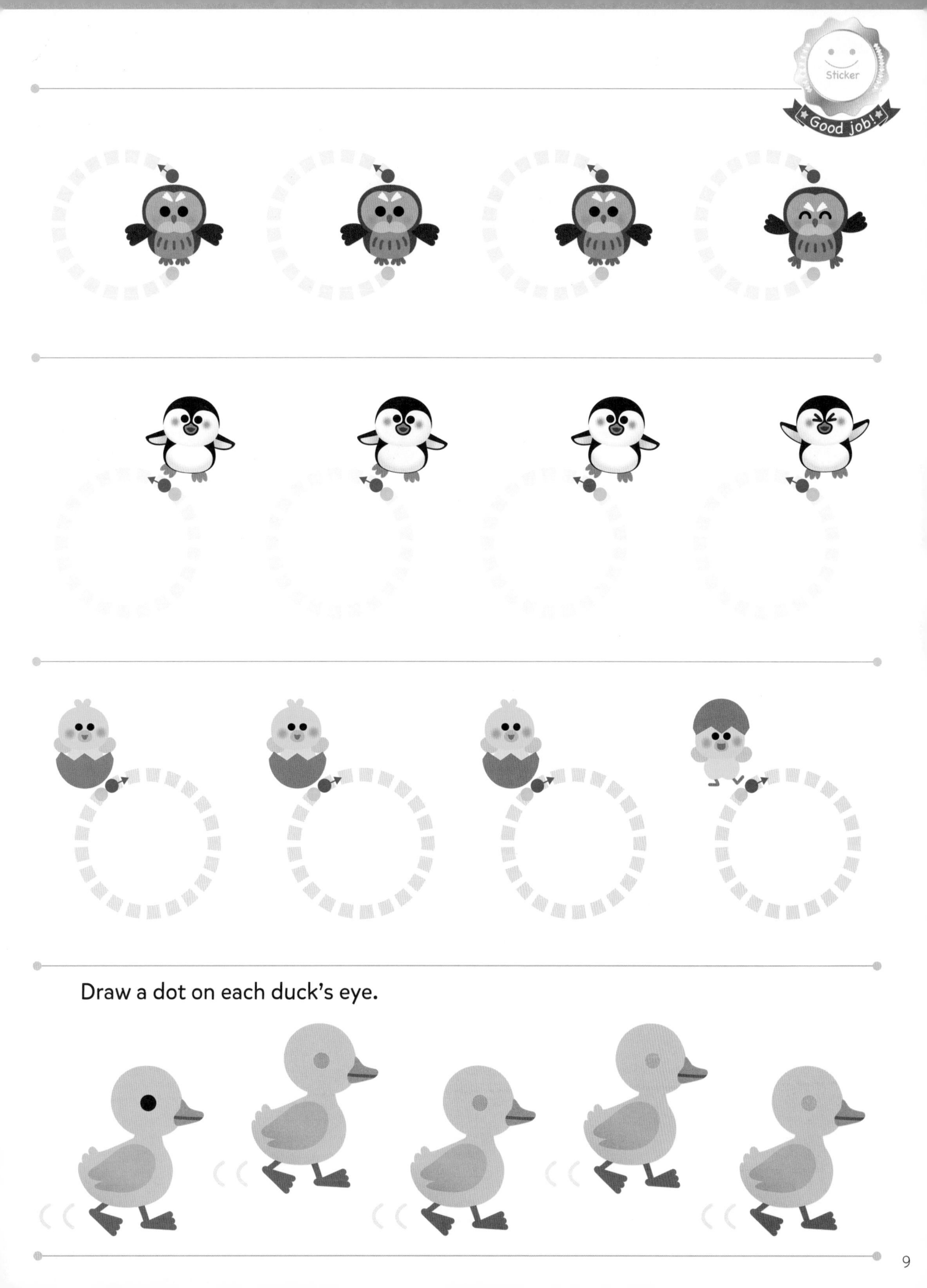
Sticker
Good job!
Draw a dot on each duck's eye.

Trace the lines from ●→ to ●.

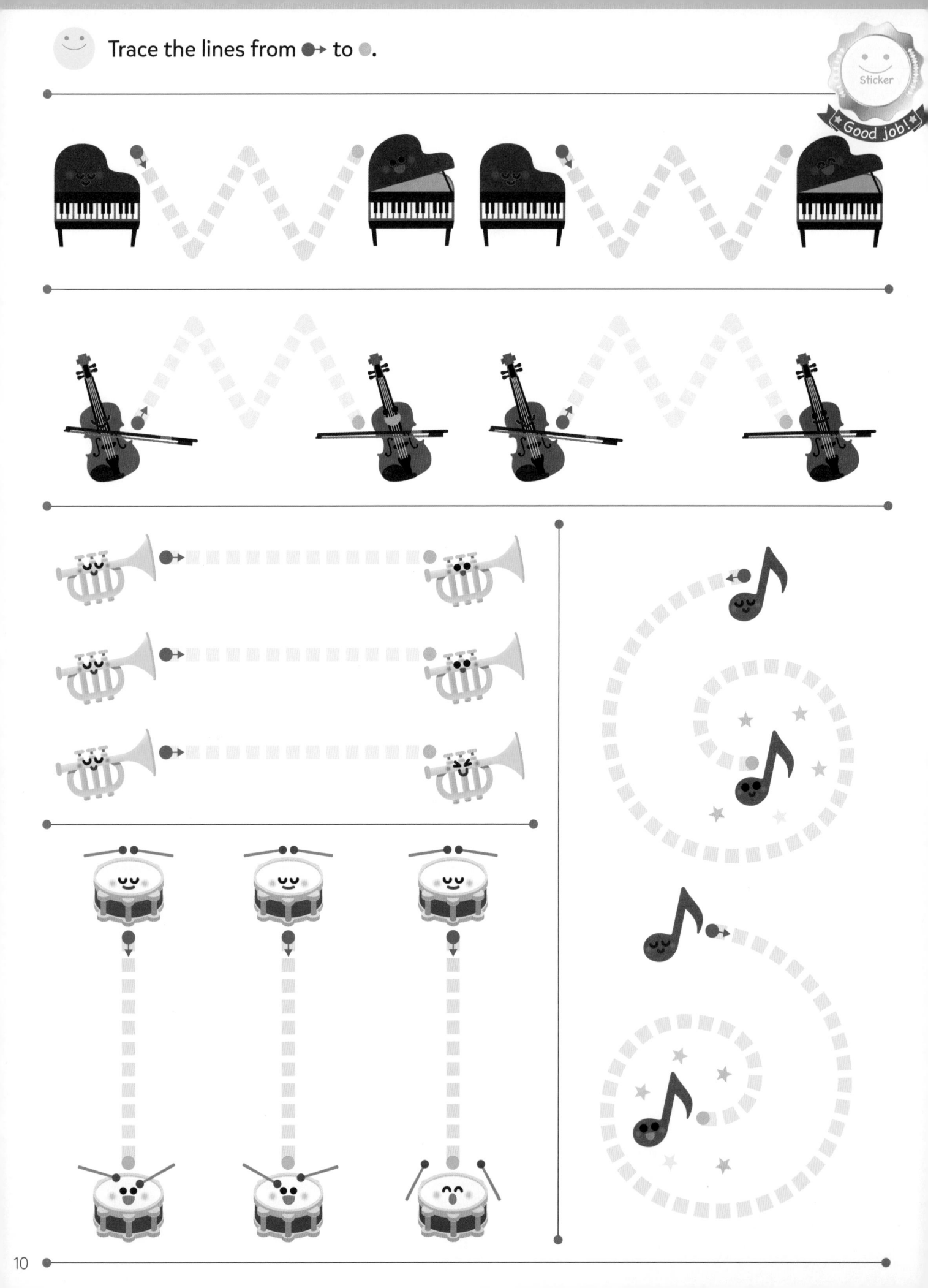

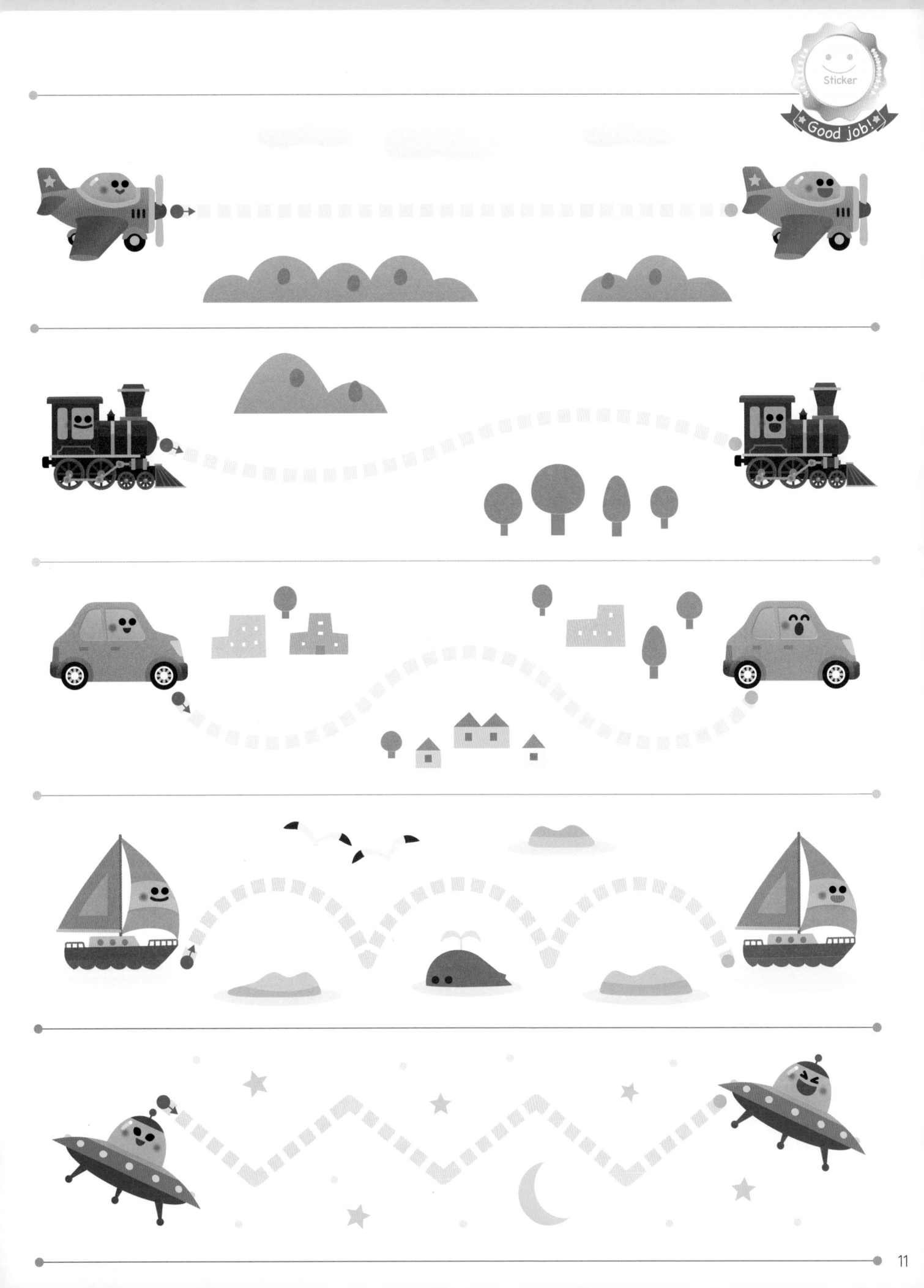
Sticker
Good job!

Letters Trace each letter.

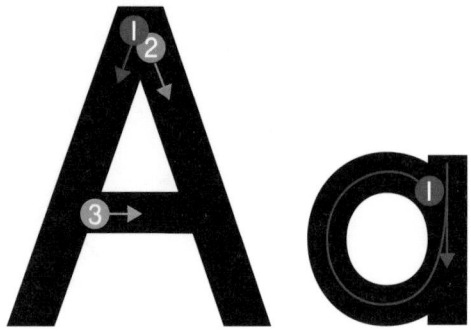

To Parents: The letter A is one of the trickiest letters to write. Encourage your child to focus on the dot at the top of the A. Both lines that go downward need to touch that dot. Then, draw a line across, connecting both sides like a bridge.

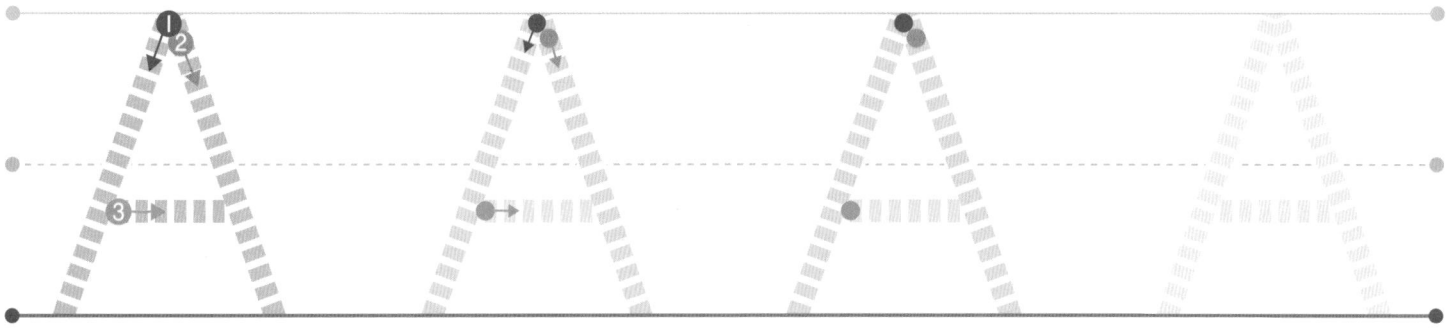

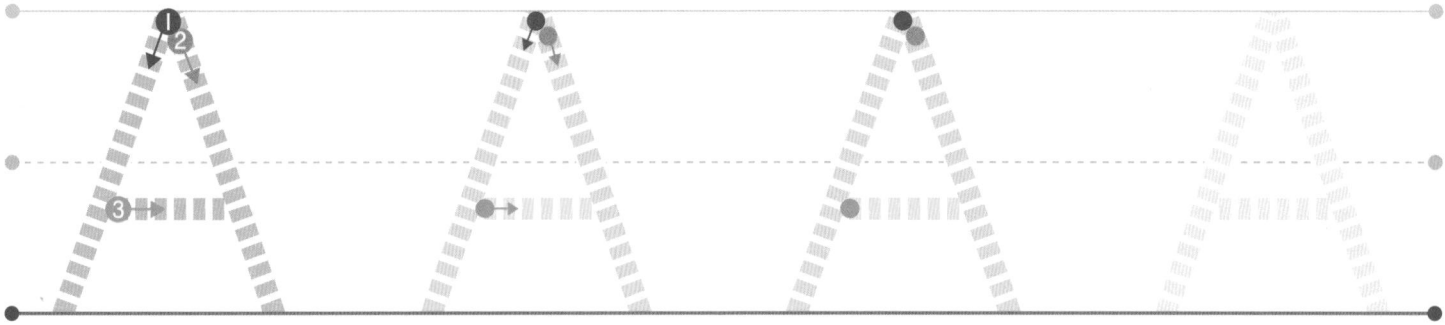

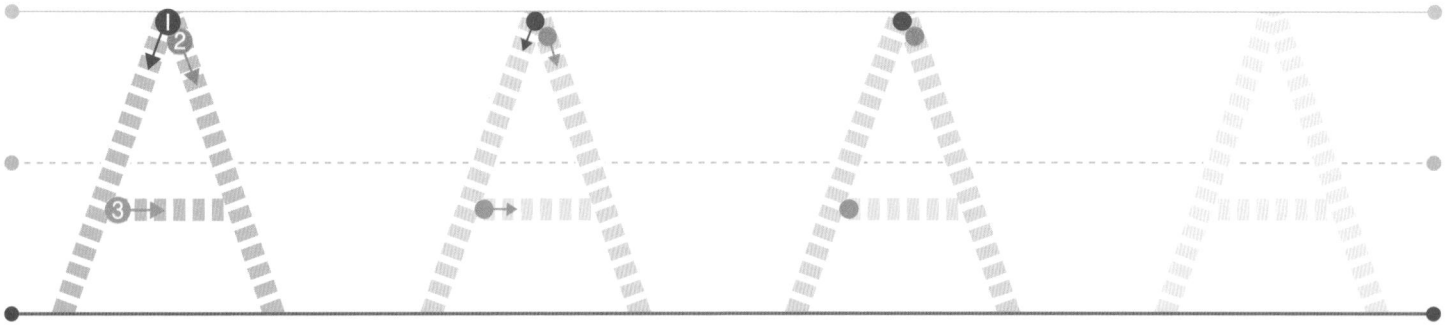

alligator
ant
apple
airplane
alligator

To Parents: The letter B is made with a straight line down, a loop to the middle, and a loop to the bottom. Remind your child that the first loop should touch the middle of the straight line. The second loop should touch the bottom of the straight line. To make it more fun, you might refer to the loops as "bellies" of the B.

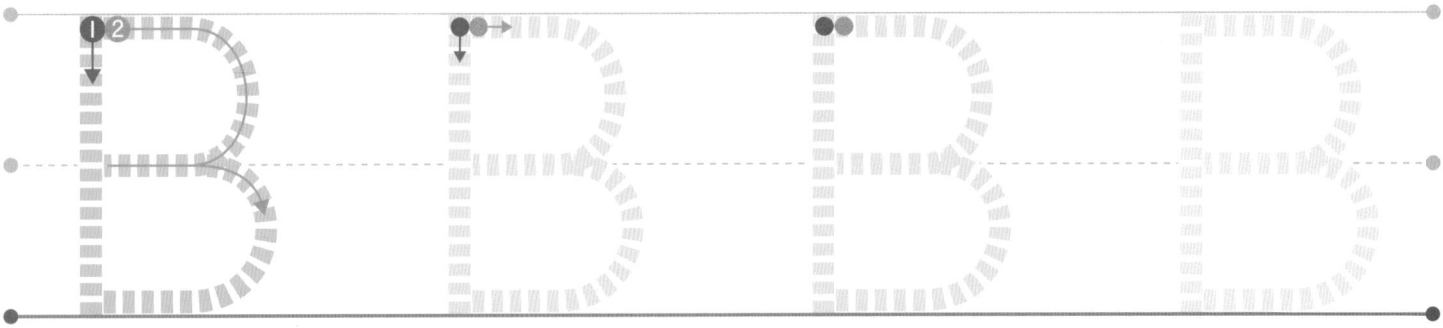

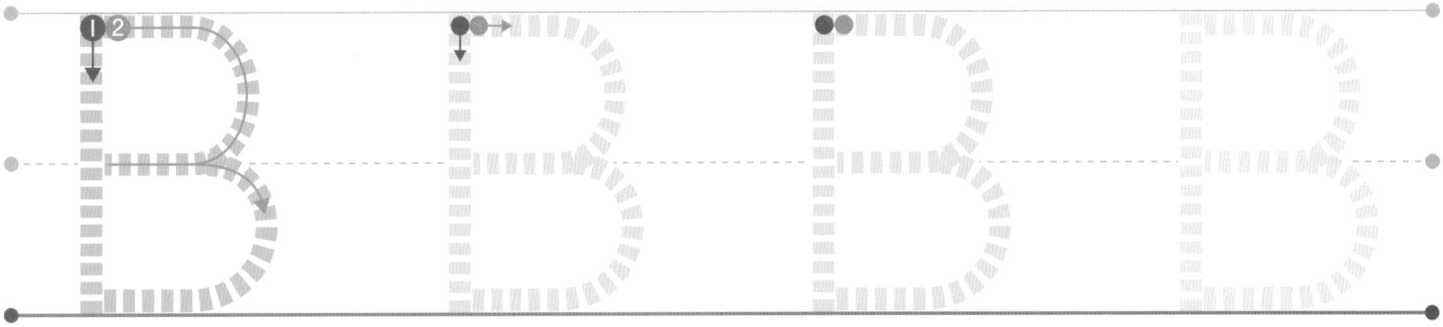

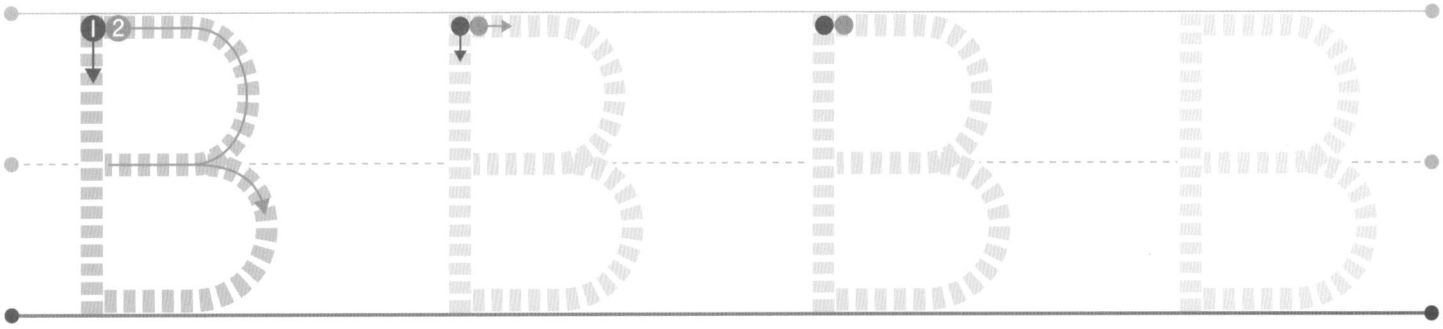

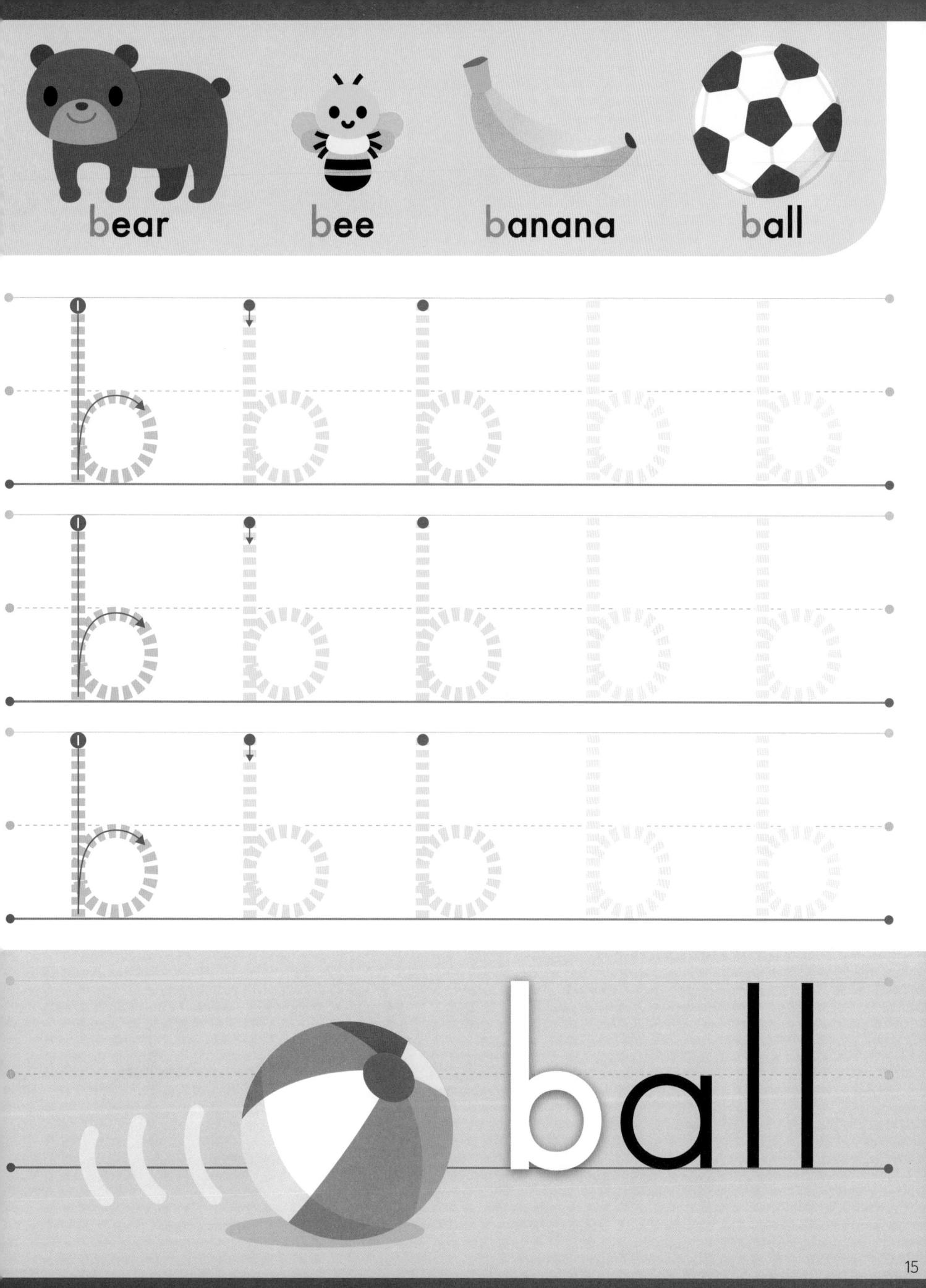
bear
bee
banana
ball
ball

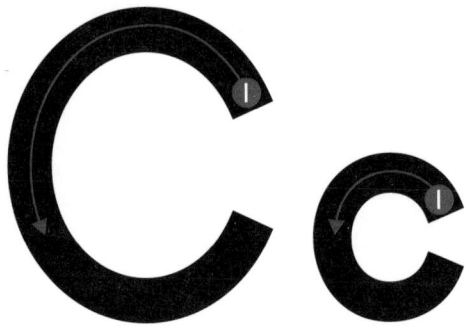

To Parents: Have your child describe what each letter looks like to them. For example, a C has a curve that looks like a crescent moon. C also has an opening that looks like a mouth. Encourage your child to think about the direction of the C by telling them that C's mouth opens toward the letter after it.

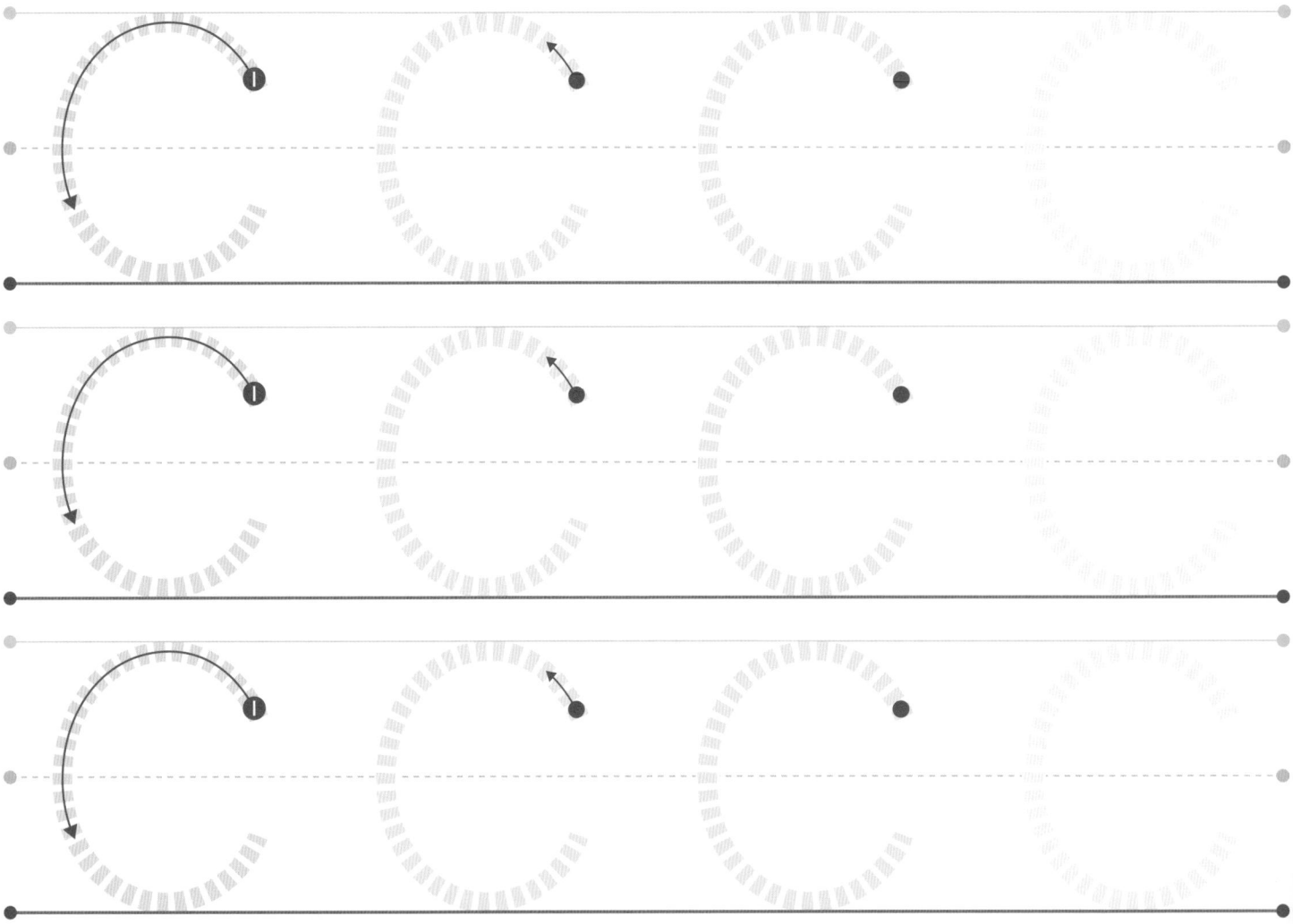

cat
cake
carrot
car

carrot

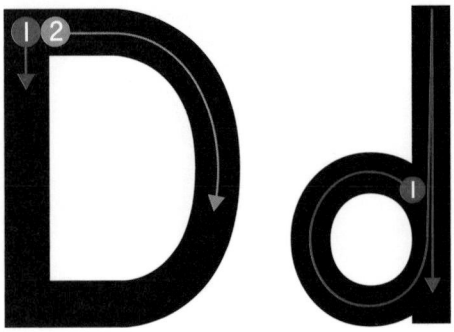

To Parents: The letter D is made with two strokes—a straight line and a loop that starts at the top of the straight line and goes to the bottom of the straight line. Ask your child to compare how the strokes for uppercase B and uppercase D are similar and different.

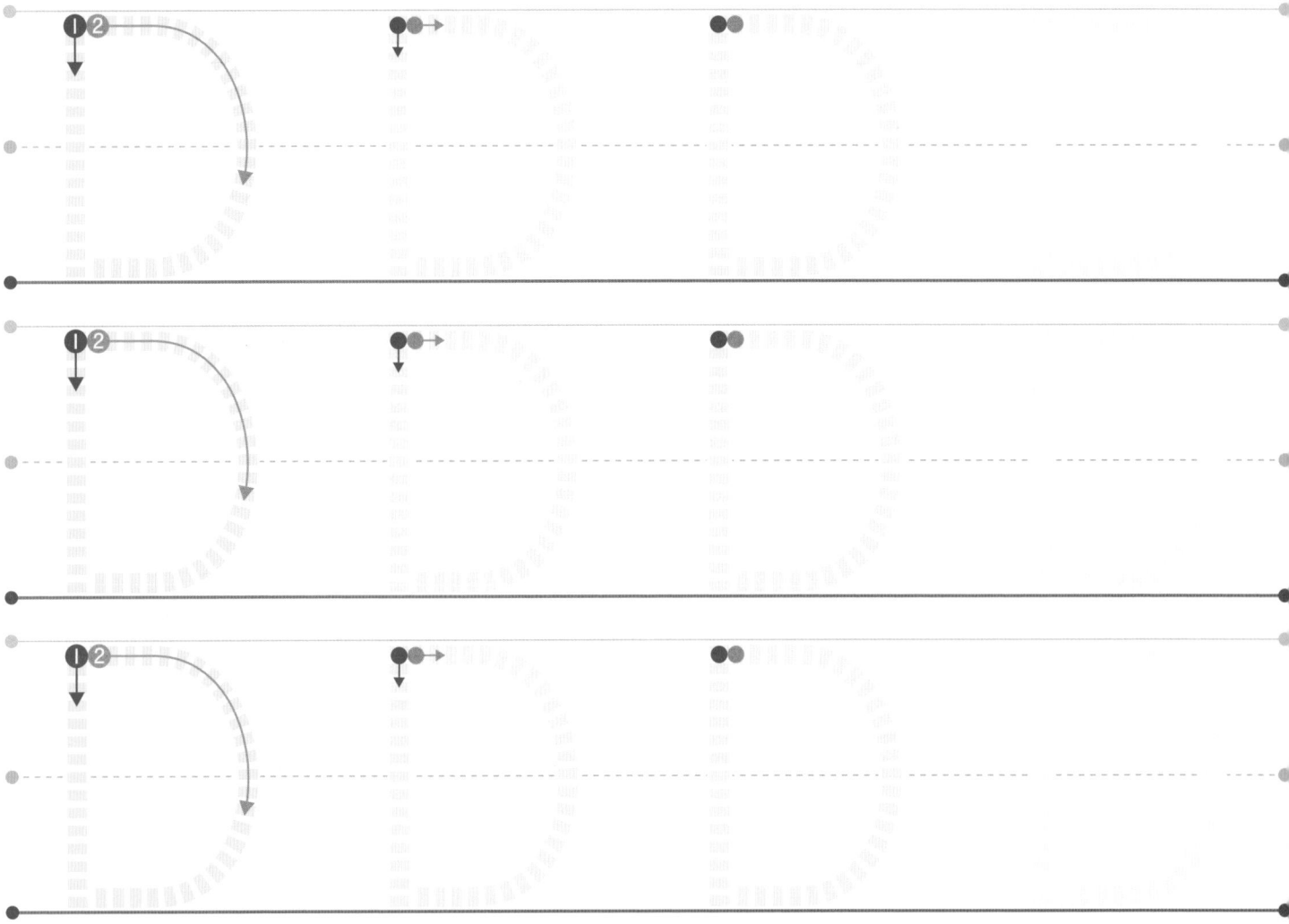

dog

duck

doughnut

drum

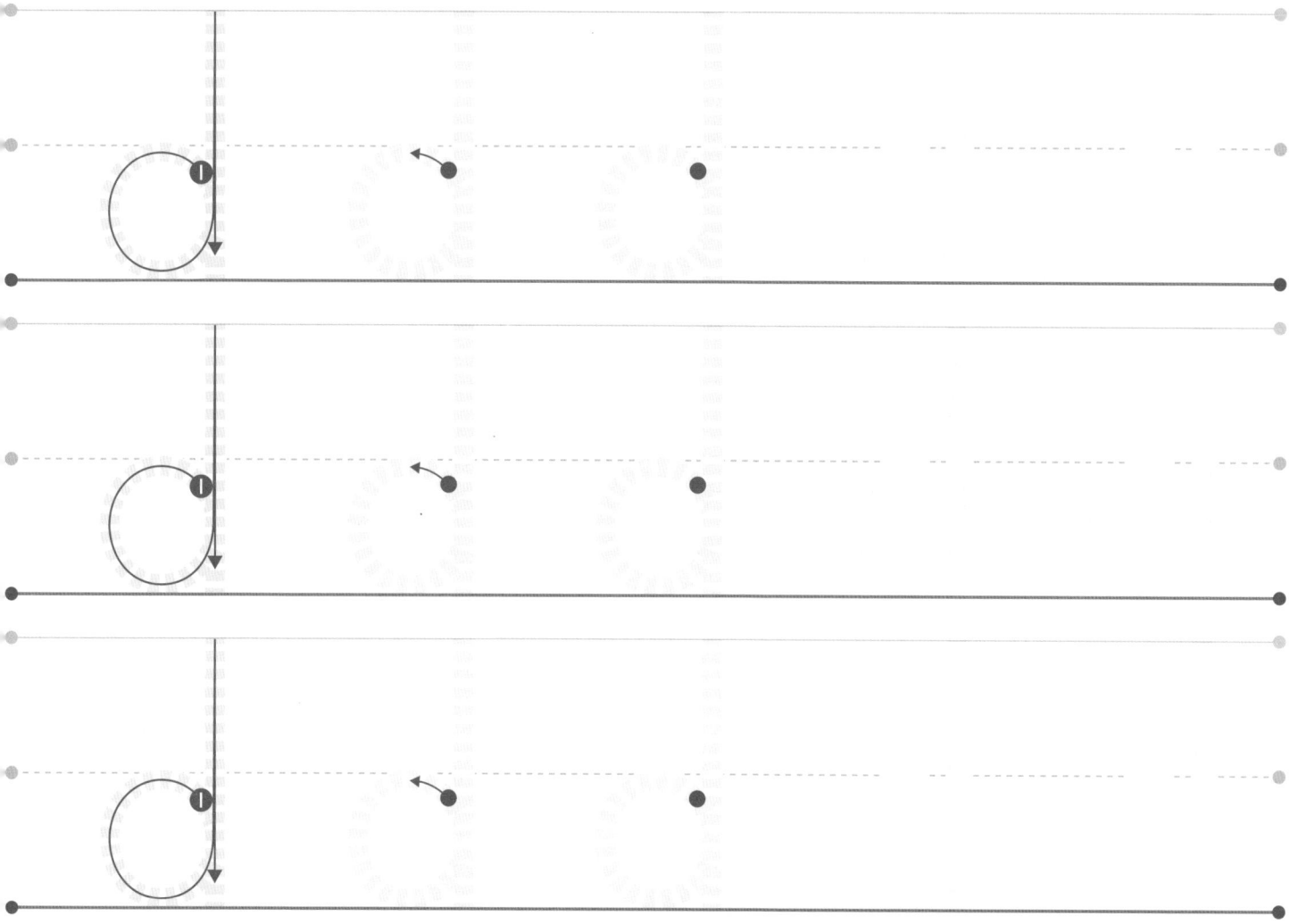

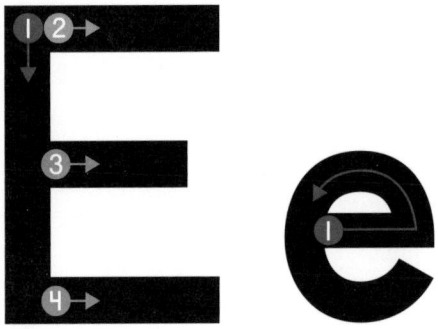

To Parents: The letter E is made with four strokes. Have your child begin with the straight line down on the left side, then count the lines across out loud –"one, two, three lines across." This will help them remember that E has three horizontal lines.

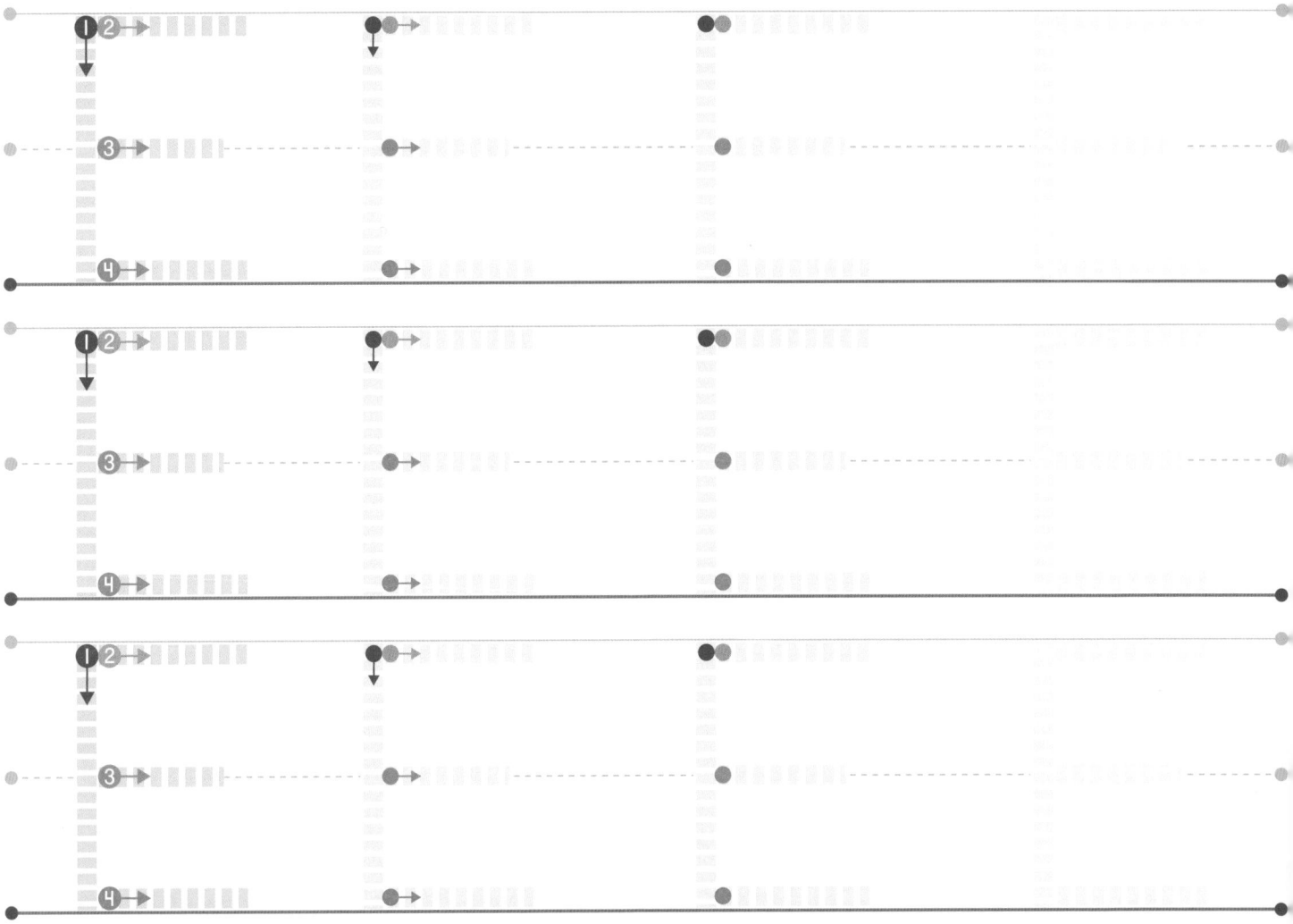

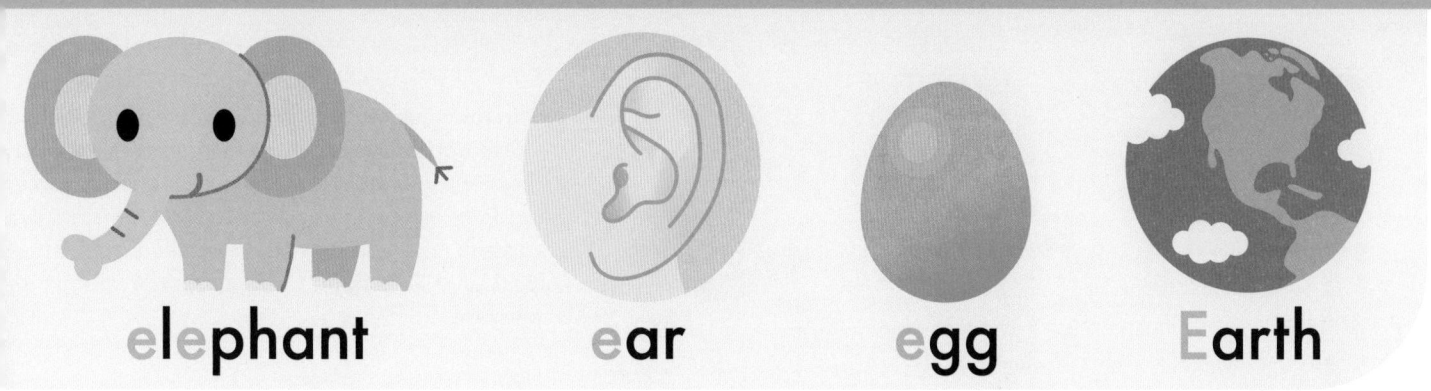
elephant
ear
egg
Earth

elephant

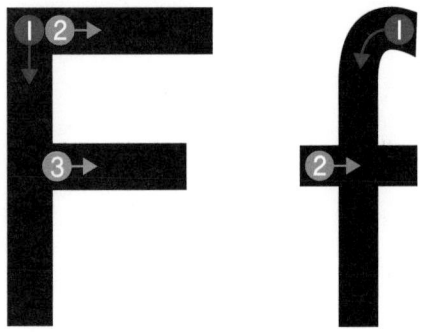

To Parents: Children often have trouble distinguishing between uppercase letters E and F, as they look very similar. Help your child notice the differences between E and F by comparing and contrasting their shapes. Discussing these differences between the letters helps your child commit the visuospatial information to memory.

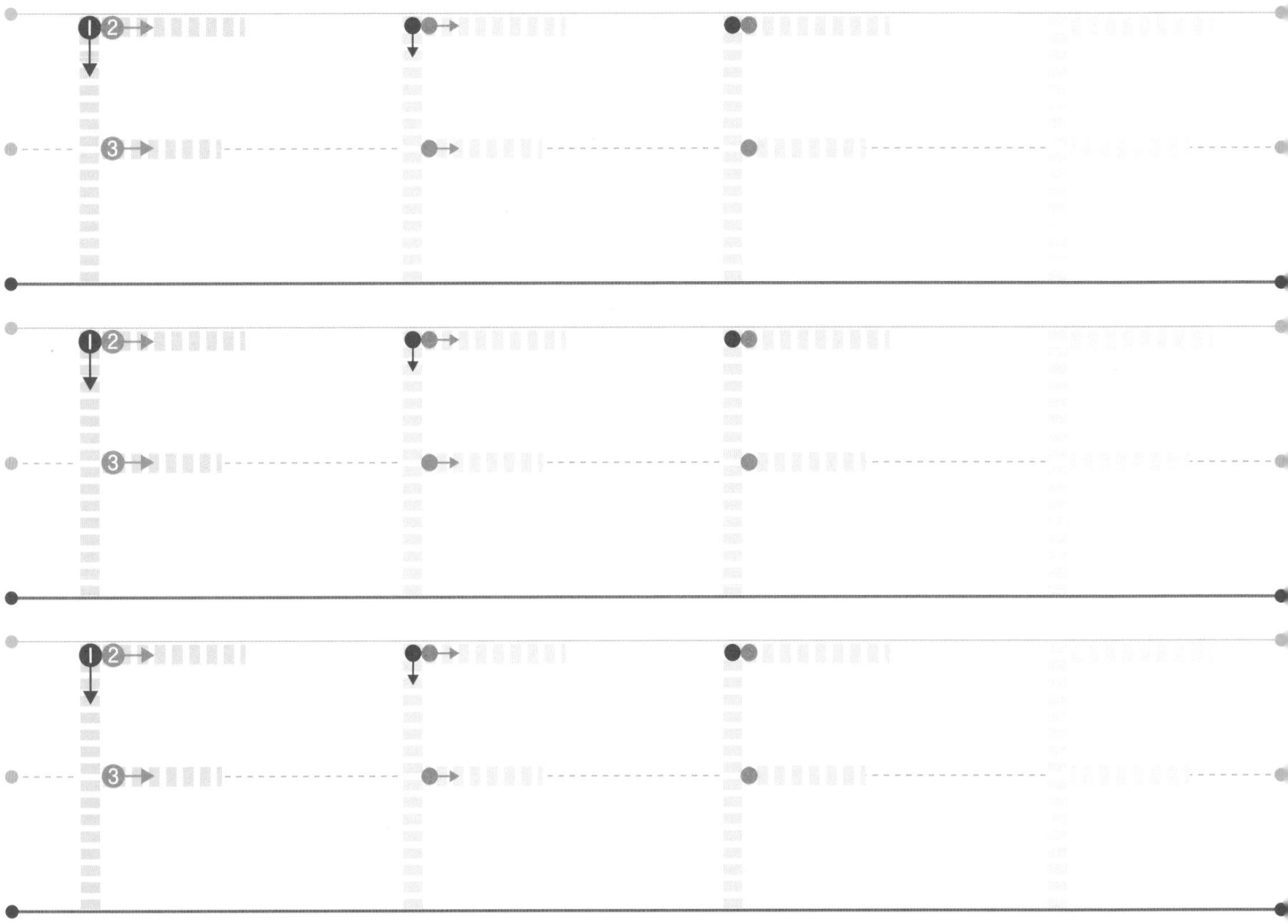

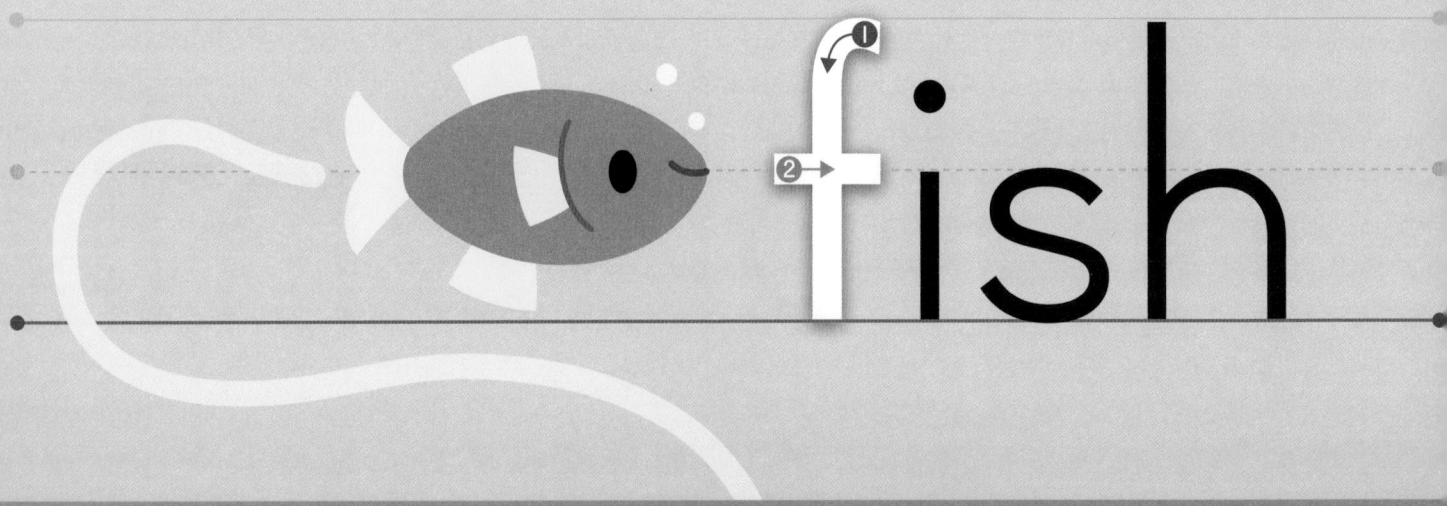

fish
flower
frog
fire engine

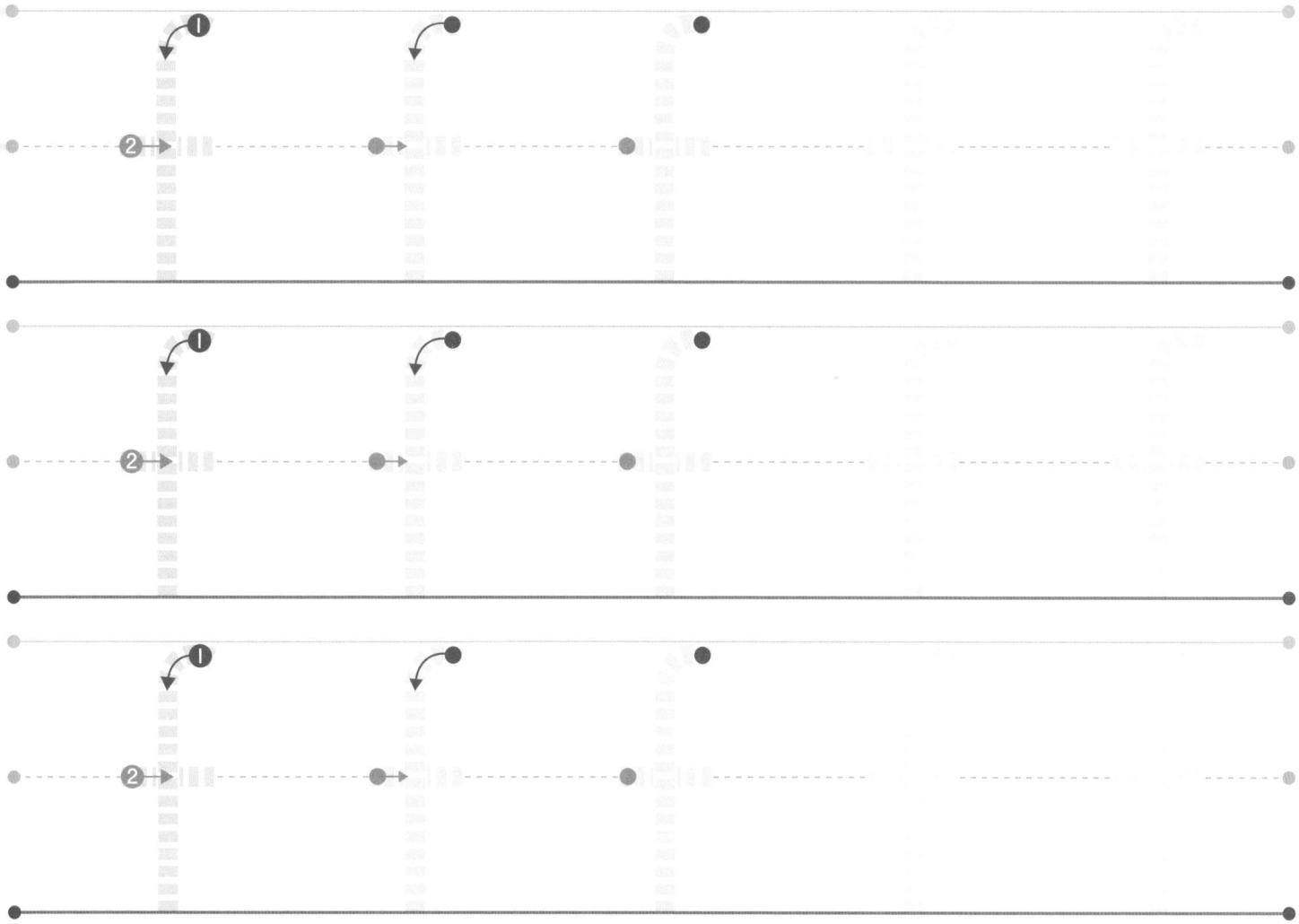

frog

To Parents: Help your child make connections between letters. Uppercase G is like the letter C but with a small line across the end of the crescent shape.

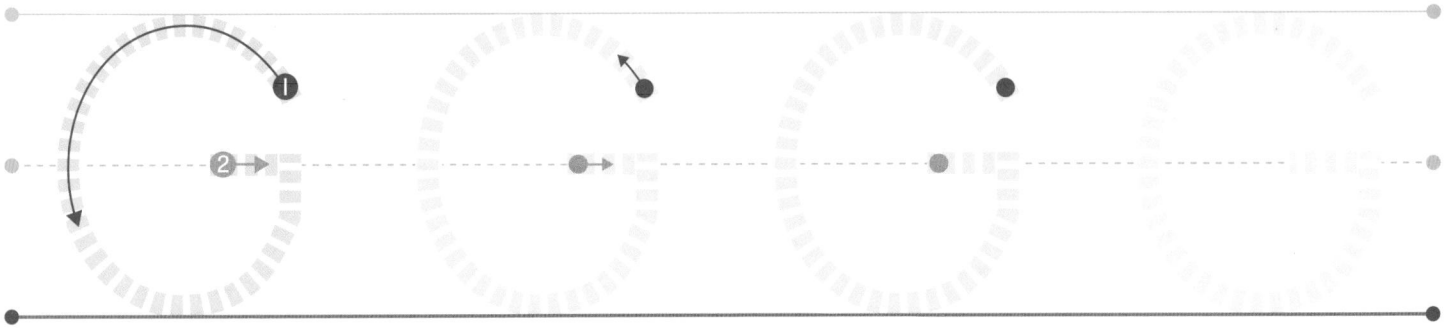

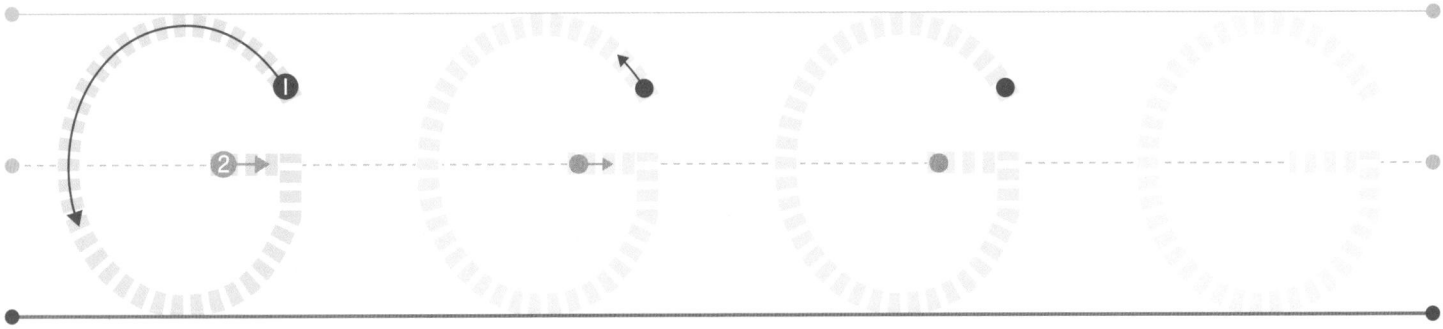

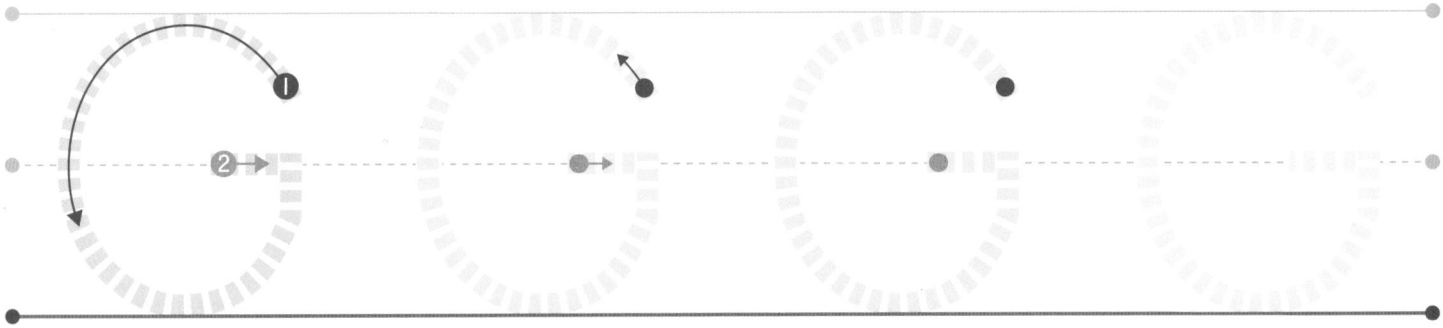

giraffe
grapes
glasses
guitar

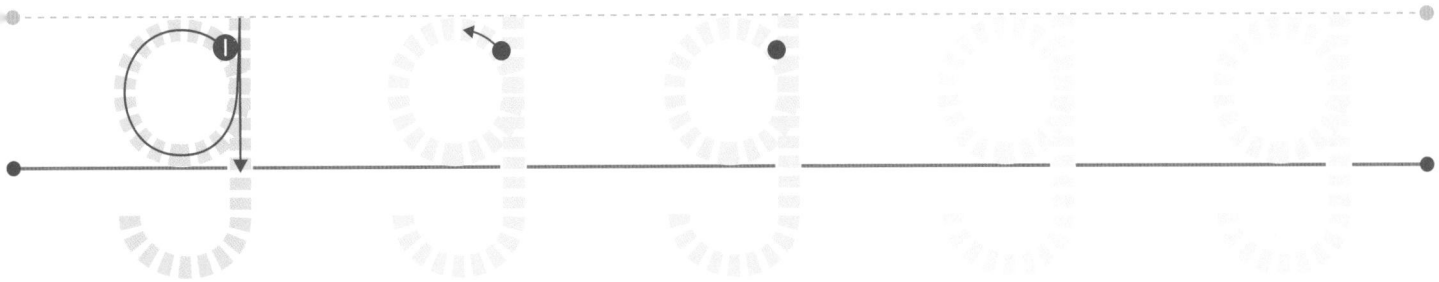

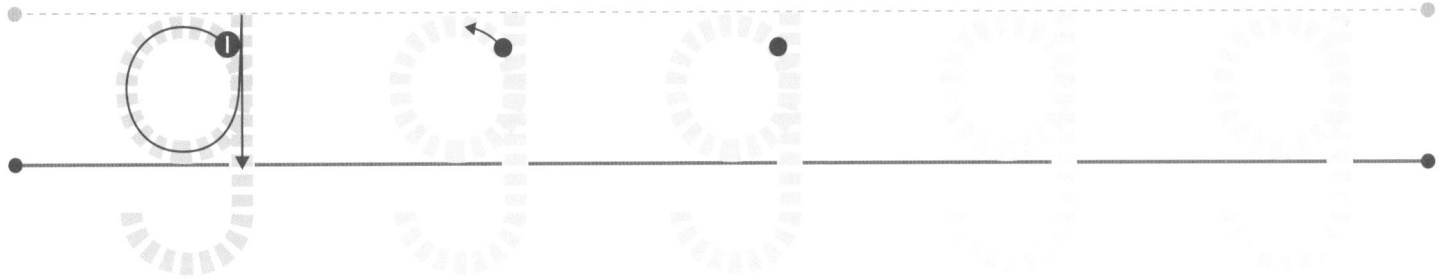

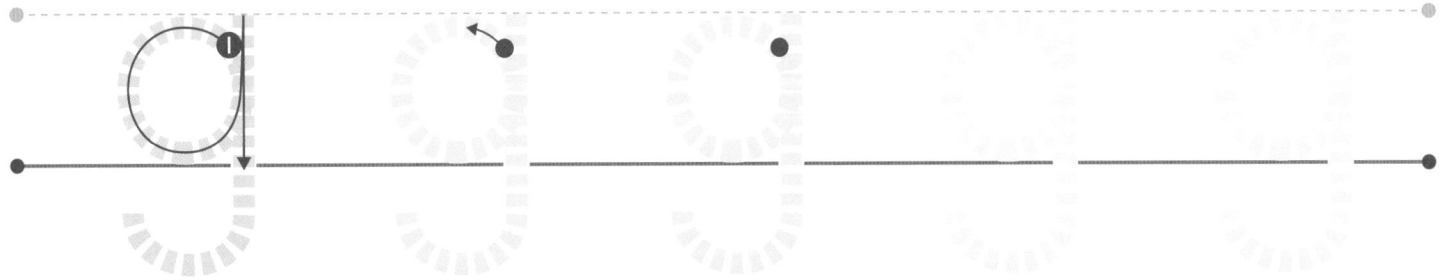

guitar

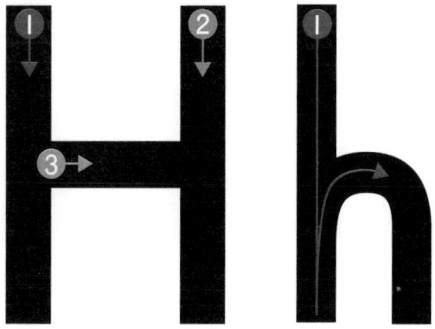

To Parents: Some children are very nervous to begin writing. Help ease their anxiety by showing them how to write the letter first. Then, ask them to trace the letter you have written.

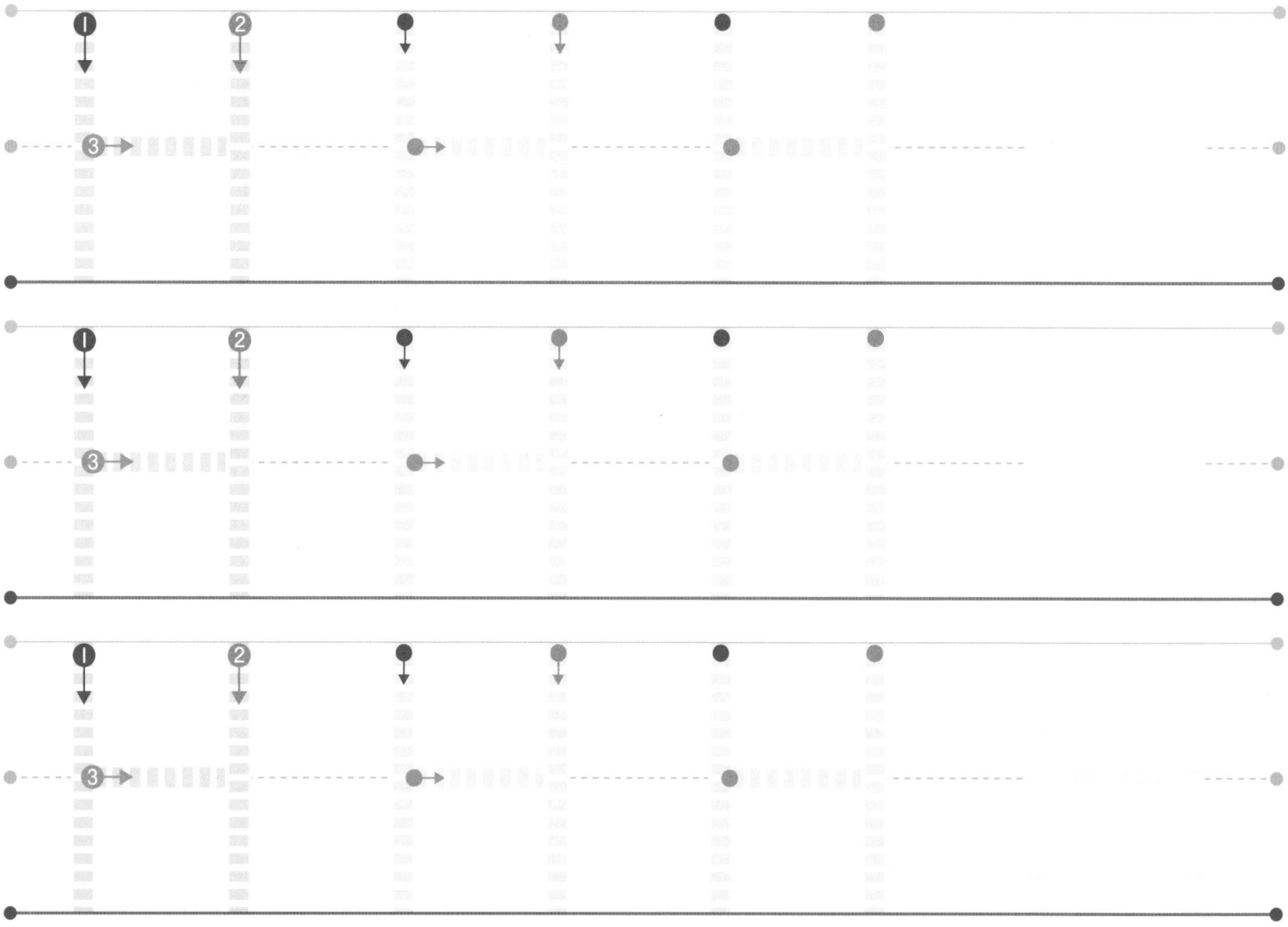

hat
horse
hedgehog
hand

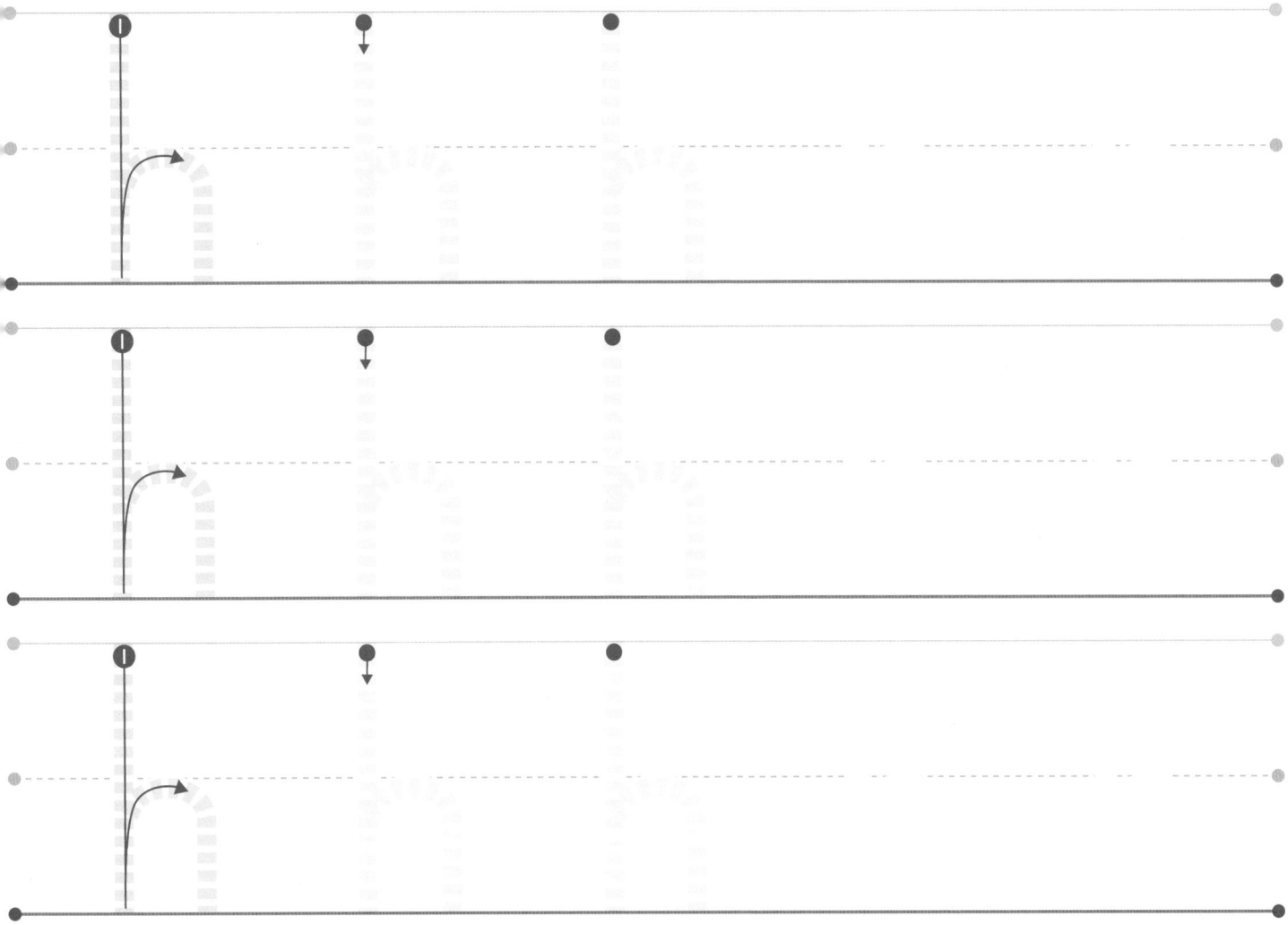

hand

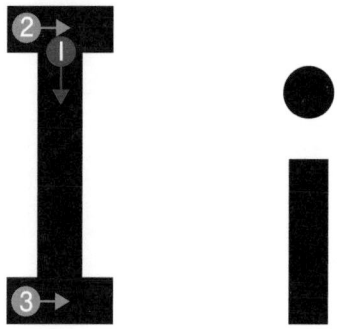

To Parents: Allow your child to use their finger to trace the letter before using a pencil. This will help orient their eyes to the shapes they are about to draw.

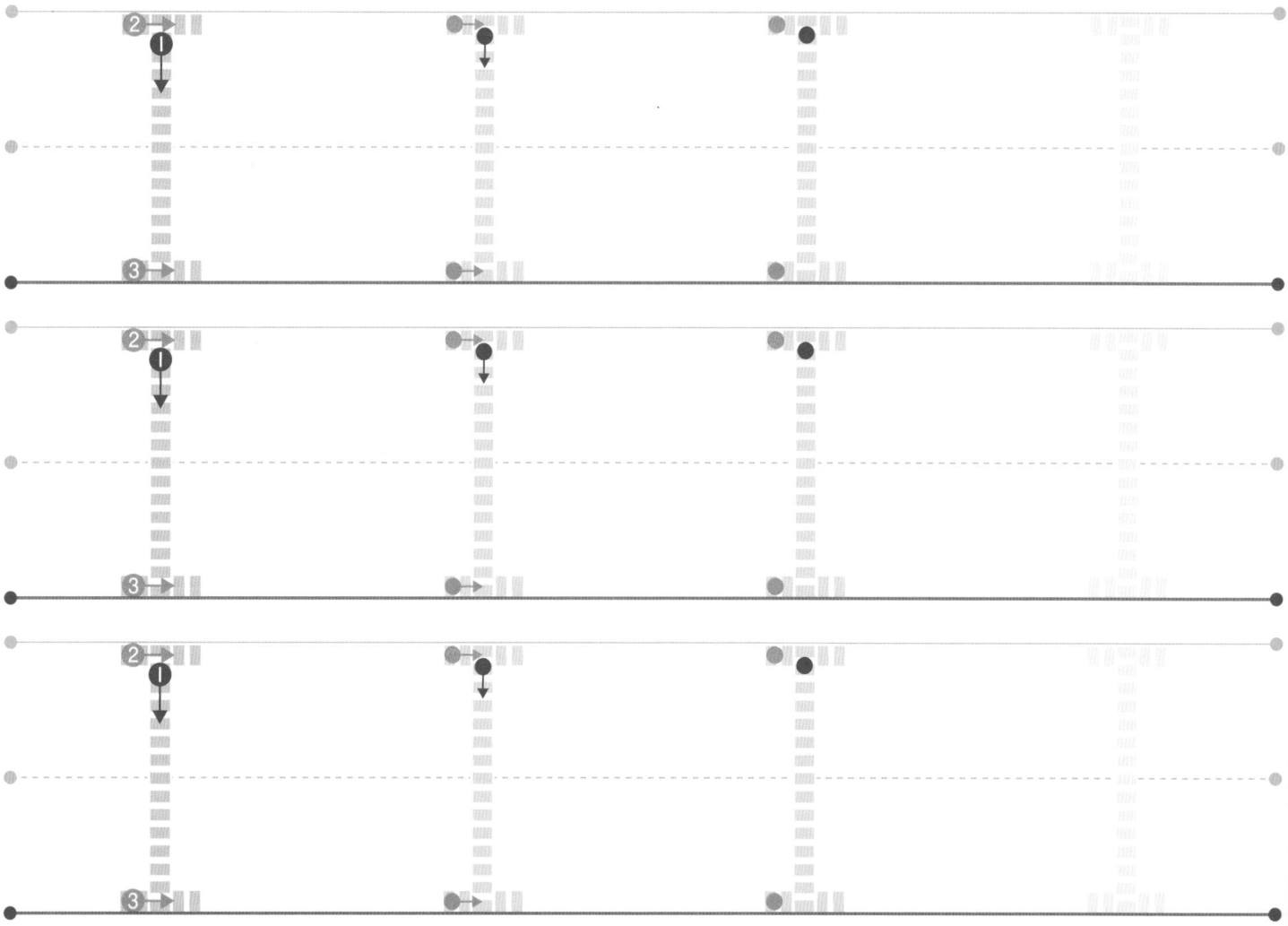

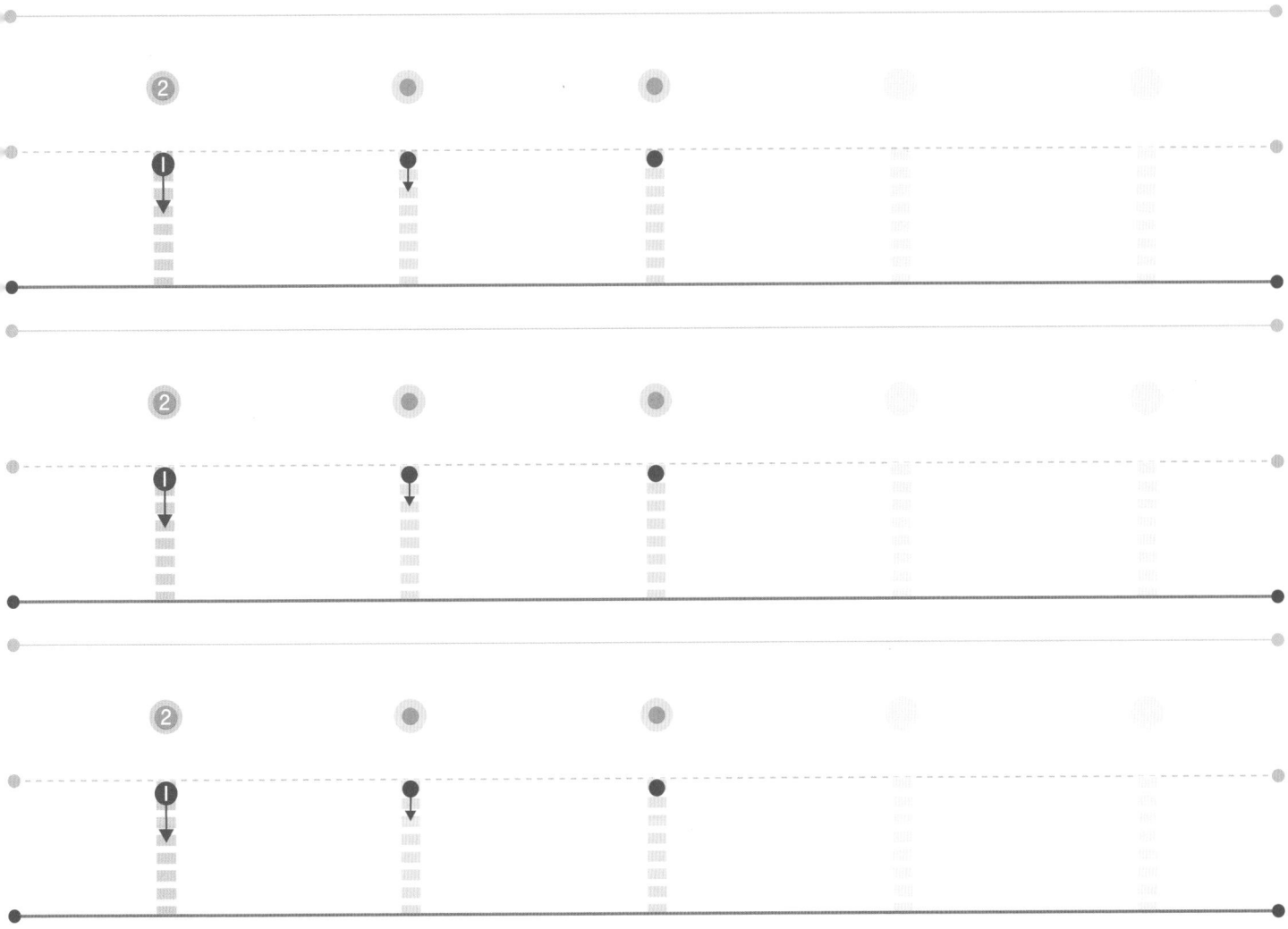

iguana

J j

To Parents: The letter J is the only uppercase letter that has a hook. J looks like the number 1 with a fishing hook on the bottom of it. Encourage your child to write a straight line down with a hook on the bottom.

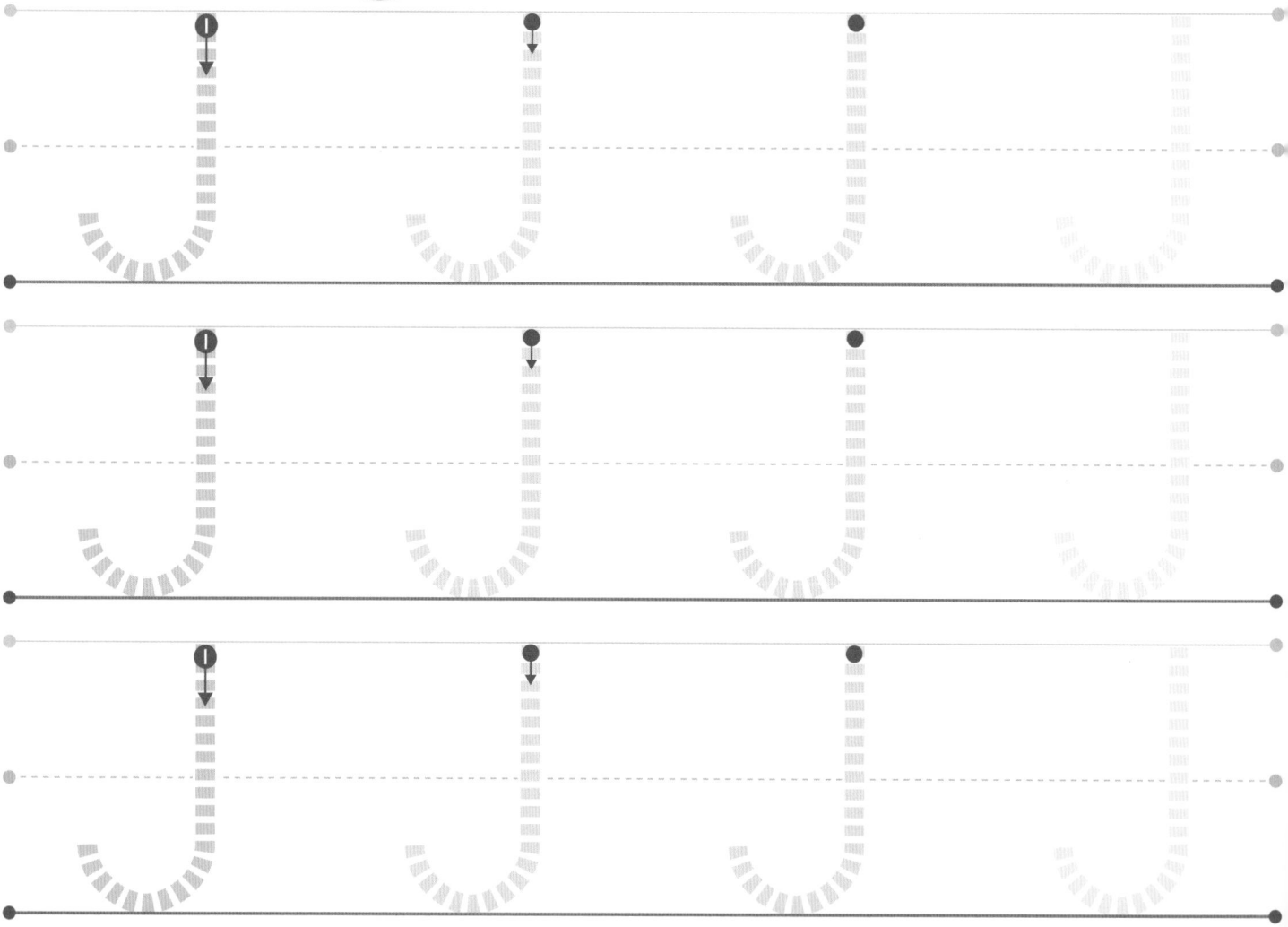

juice

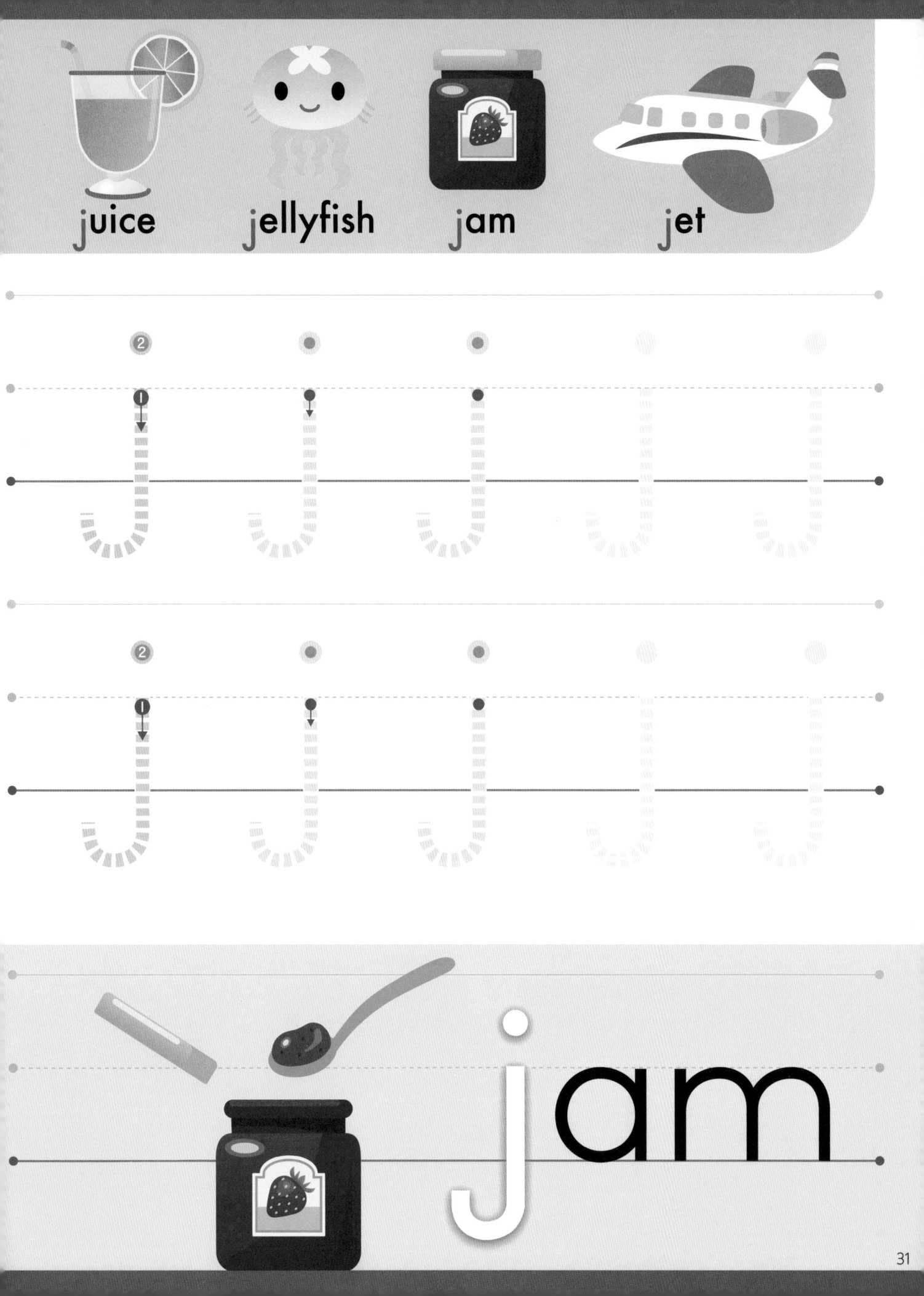
juice
jellyfish
jam
jet
jam

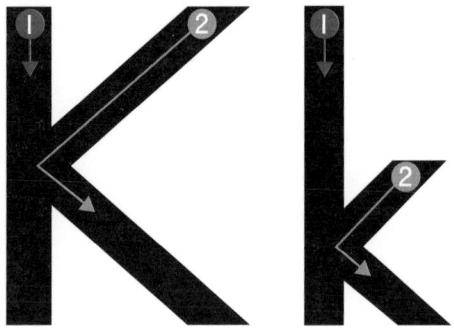

To Parents: The letter K is a very difficult letter for children to learn to write. Encourage your child to make sure that both diagonal lines meet up at the center of the straight line of the K. The diagonal line at the bottom "kicks" out.

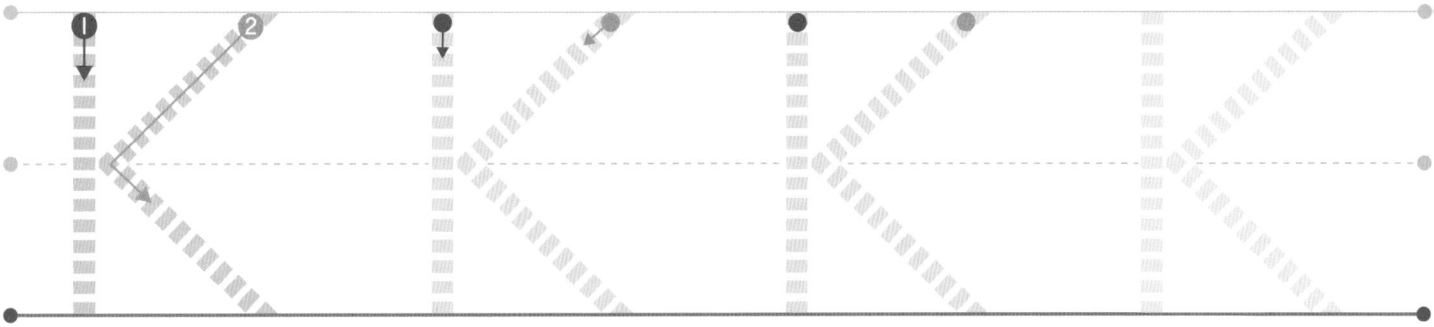

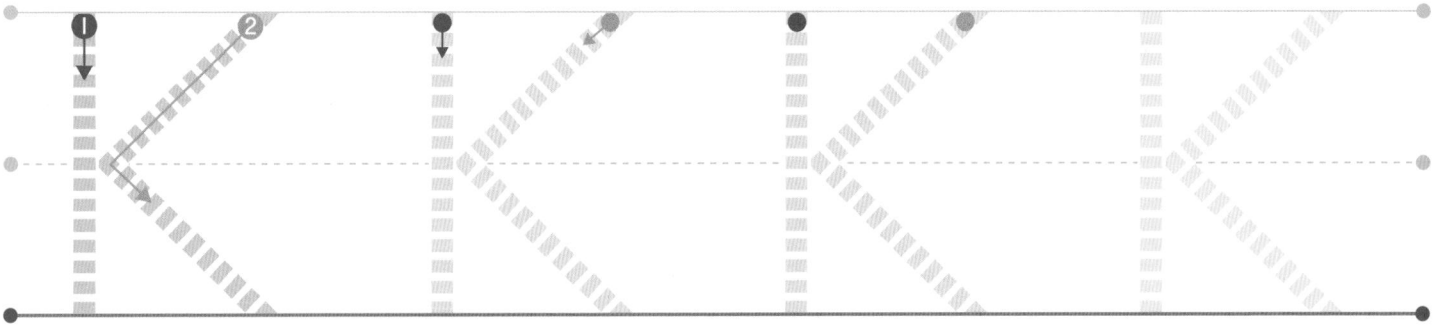

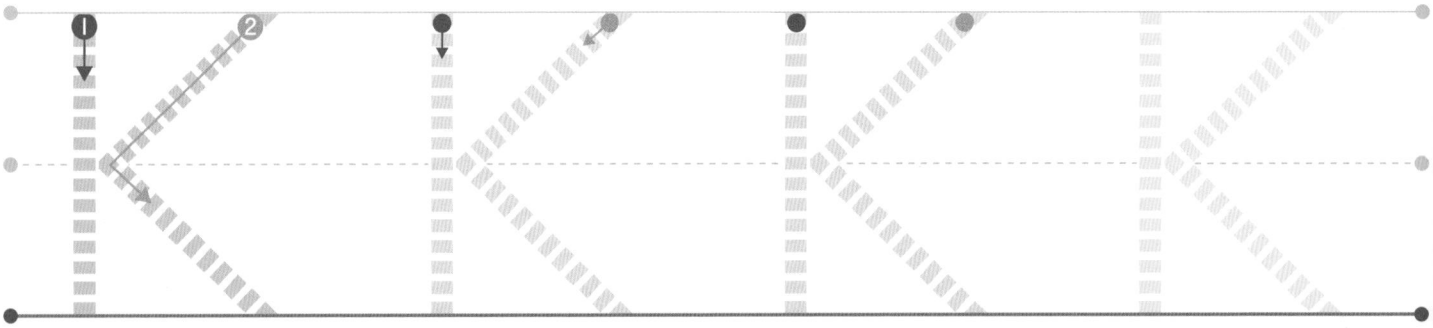

koala
kiwi
key
kite

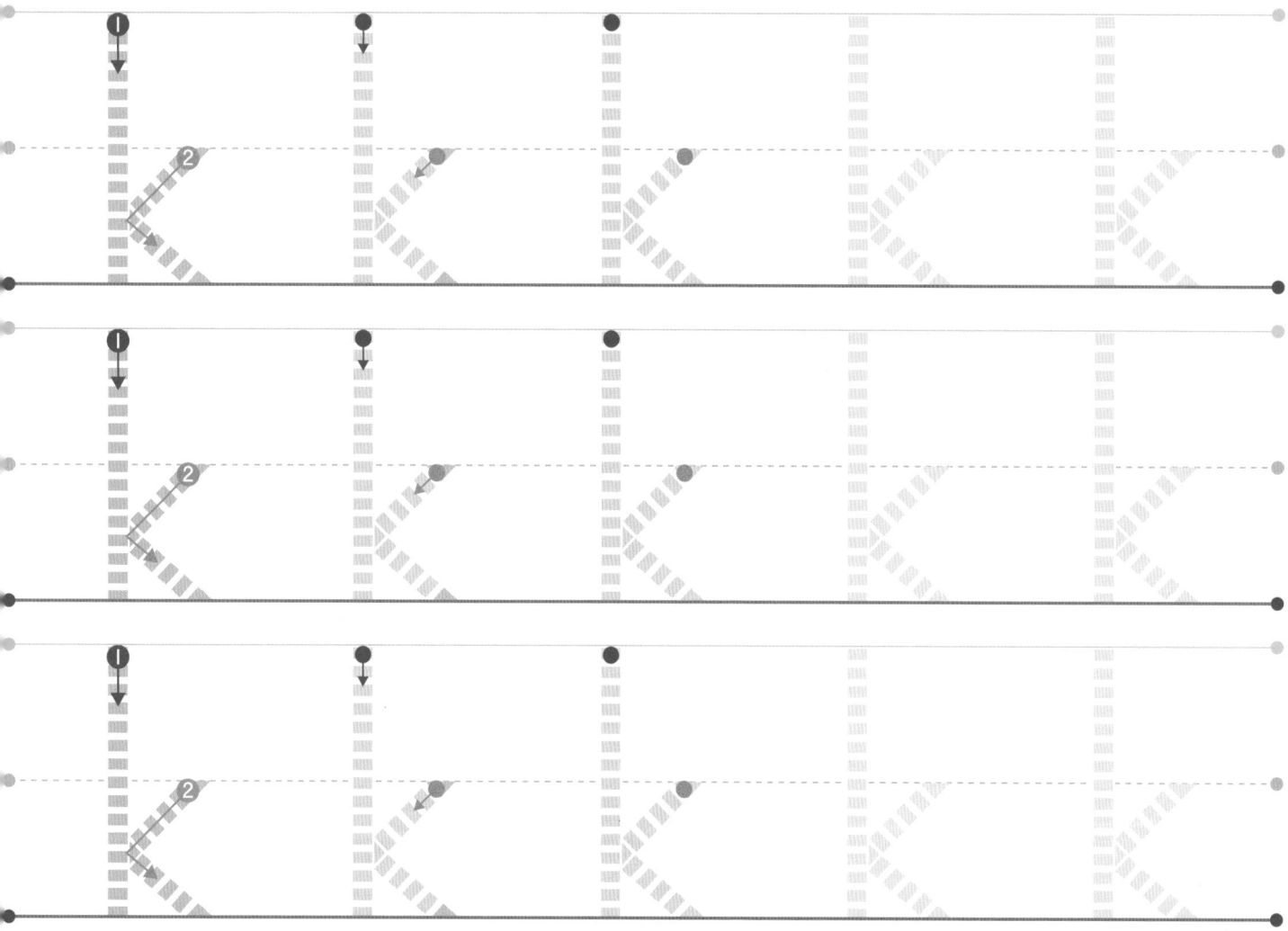

kite

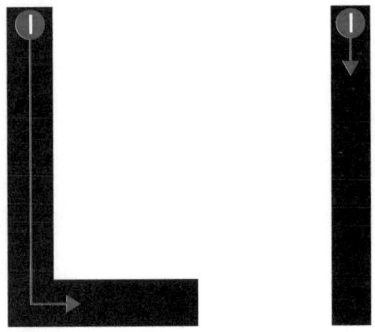

To Parents: Show your child that many letters (B, D, E, F, H, I, J, K, M, N, P, R, T) begin with a straight, vertical line down. L is no different. Start with a straight line down and then make a horizontal line across.

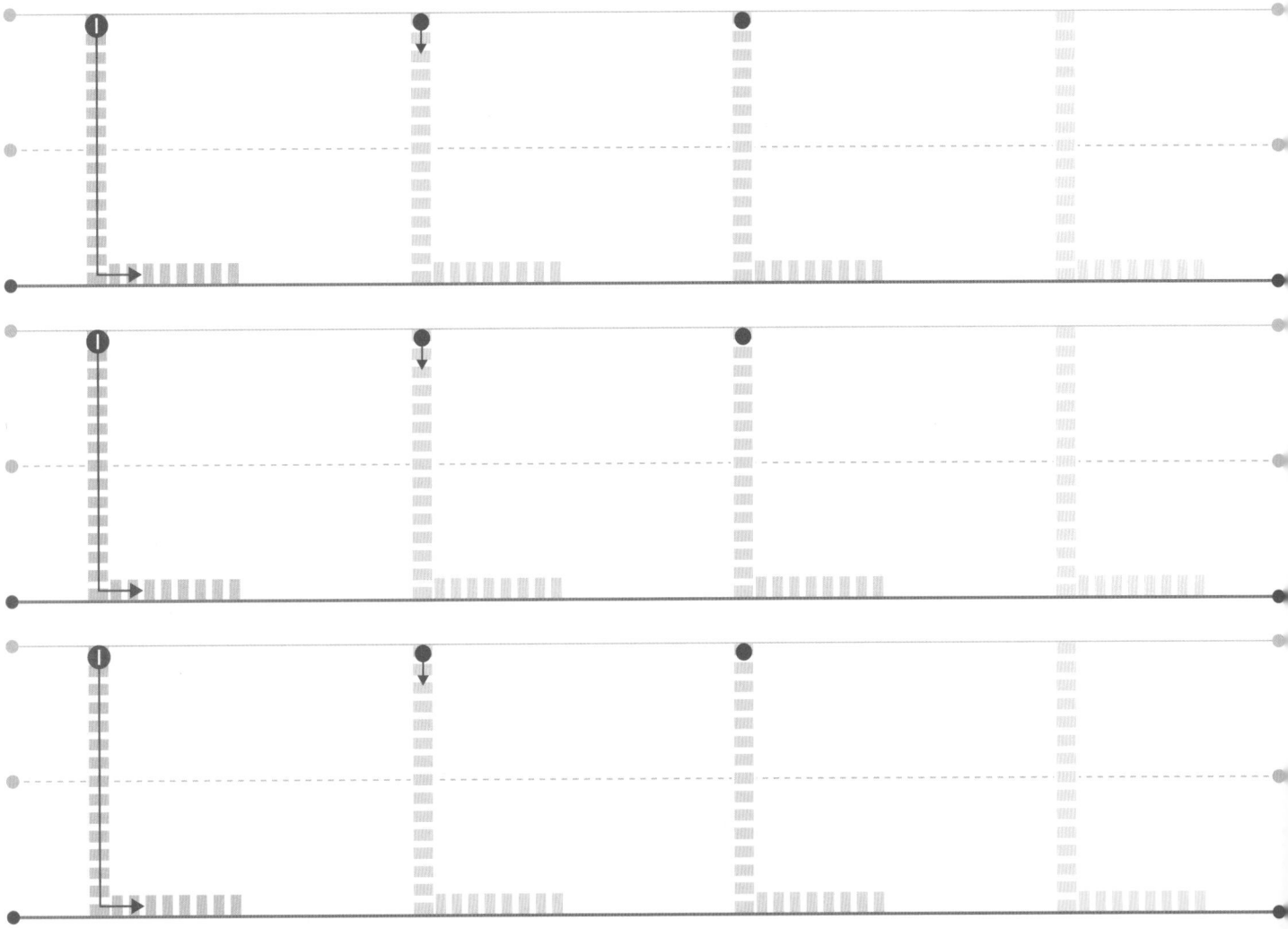

lion

lion

lemon

ladybug

leaf

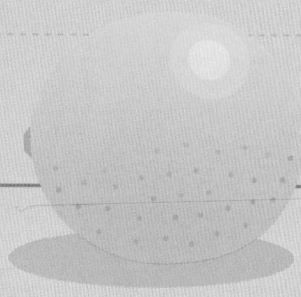

lemon

Mm

To Parents: Point out that uppercase M looks like pointed mountains, while lowercase m looks like small, rounded hills. Give your child a mantra to say as they make each letter. This will help them remember the strokes. "Down, down, up, down" could be their mantra for uppercase M.

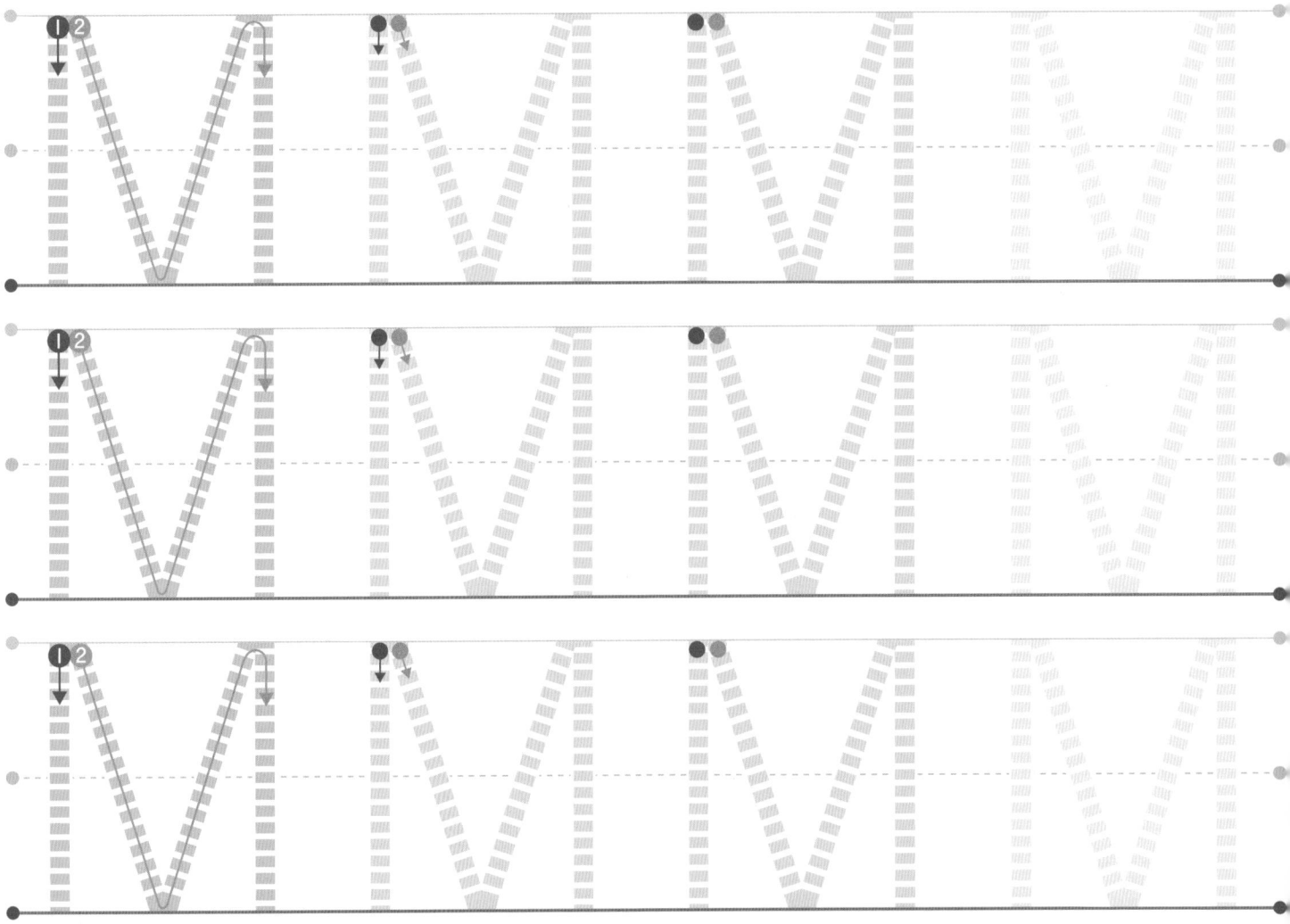

moon

monkey

mouse

milk

mouse

Nn

To Parents: All letters begin at the top of the blue line. Ensure that your child does not try to start any of the letters from the bottom.

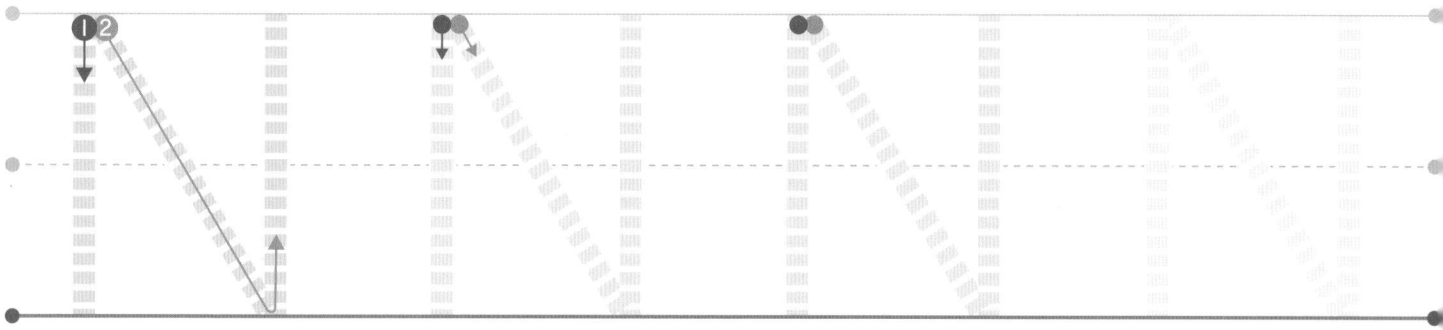

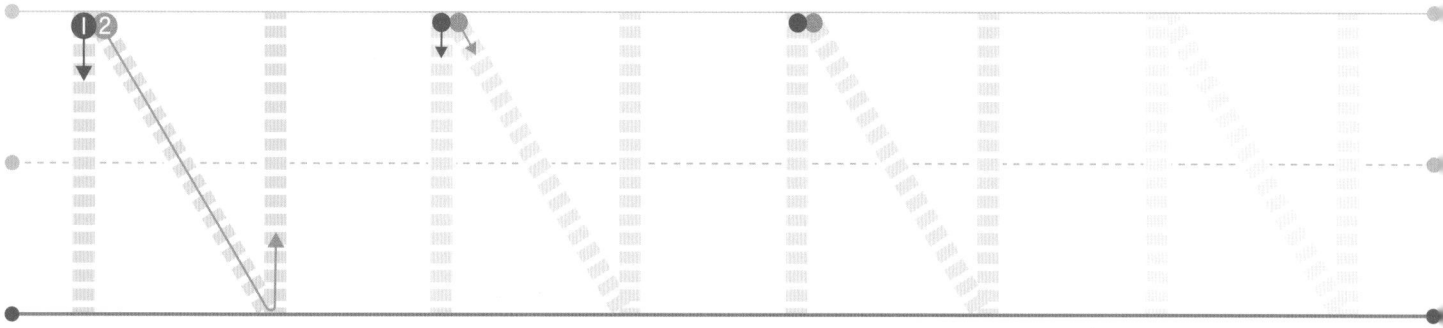

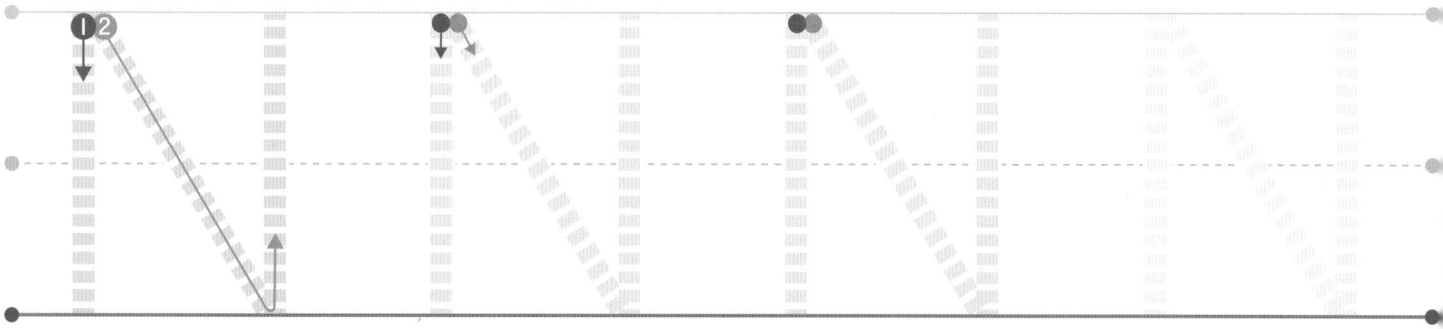

nest

night

nest

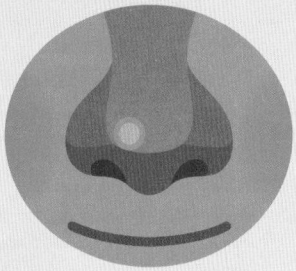

nose

necklace

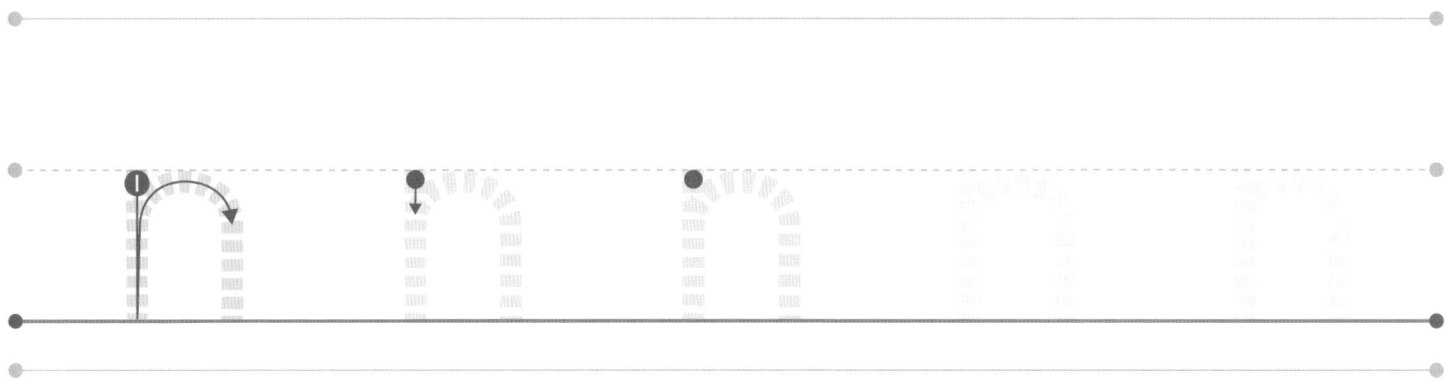

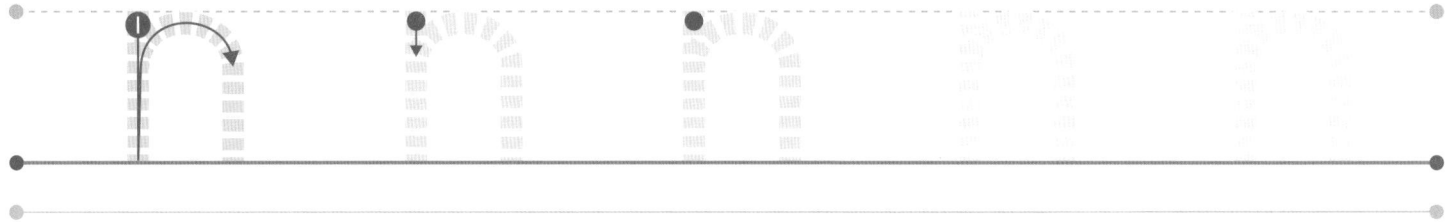

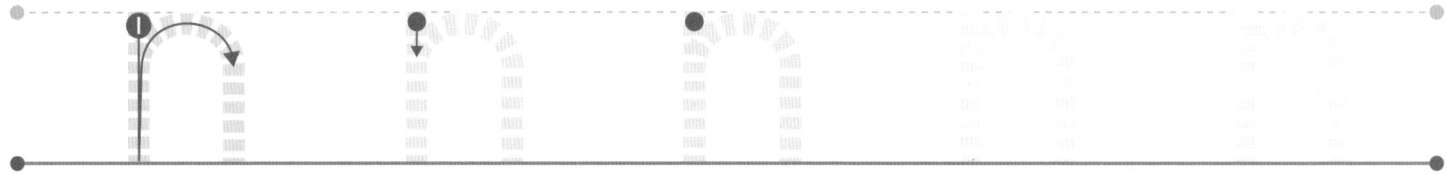

necklace

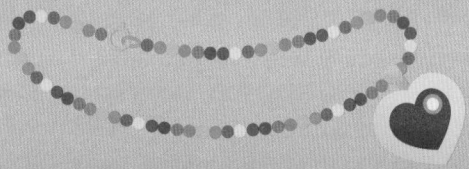

To Parents: Encourage your child to start the O at the top of the line. Then make an elongated circle. Try to help them connect both sides of the circle at the dot you began with on the top of the line.

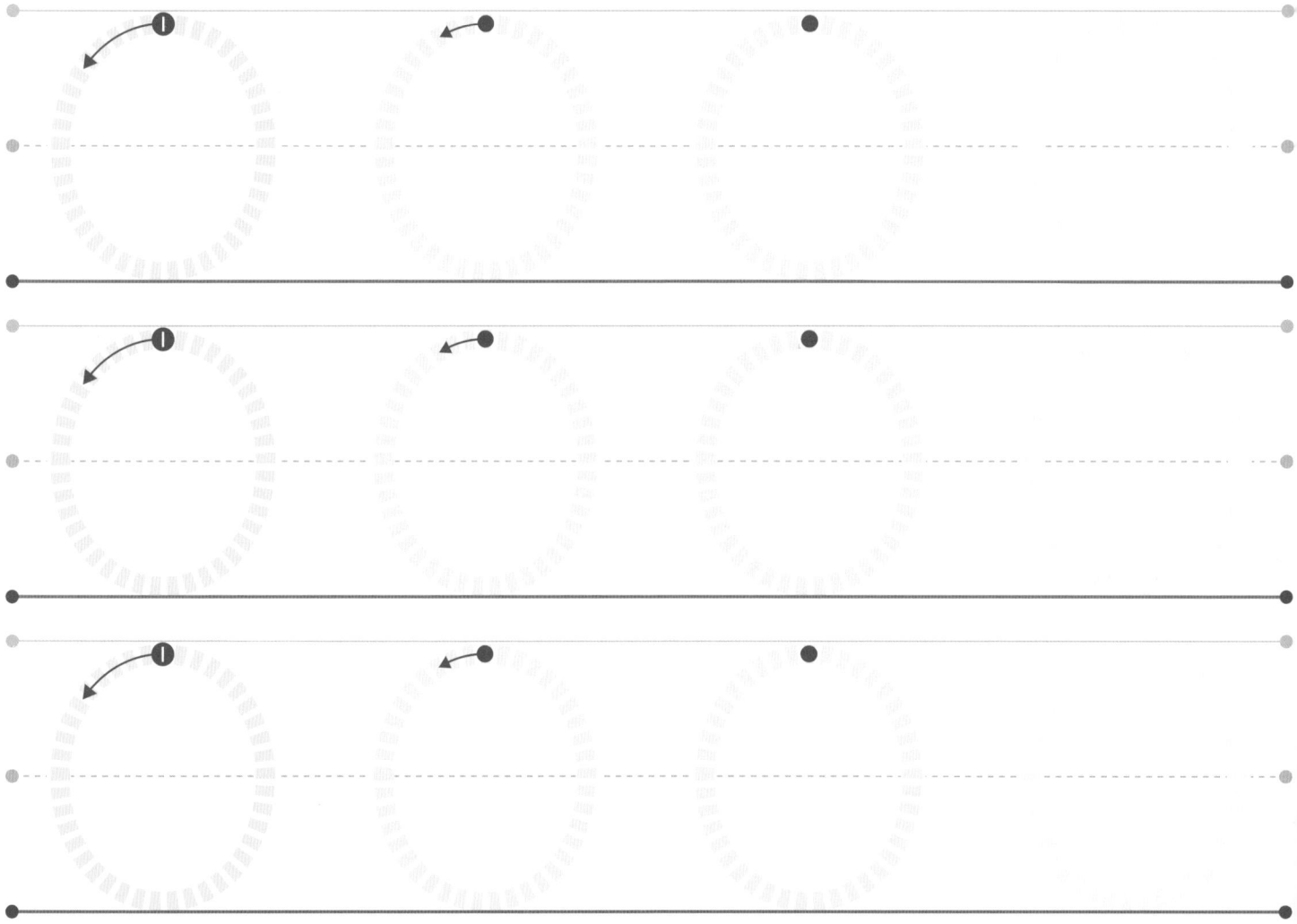

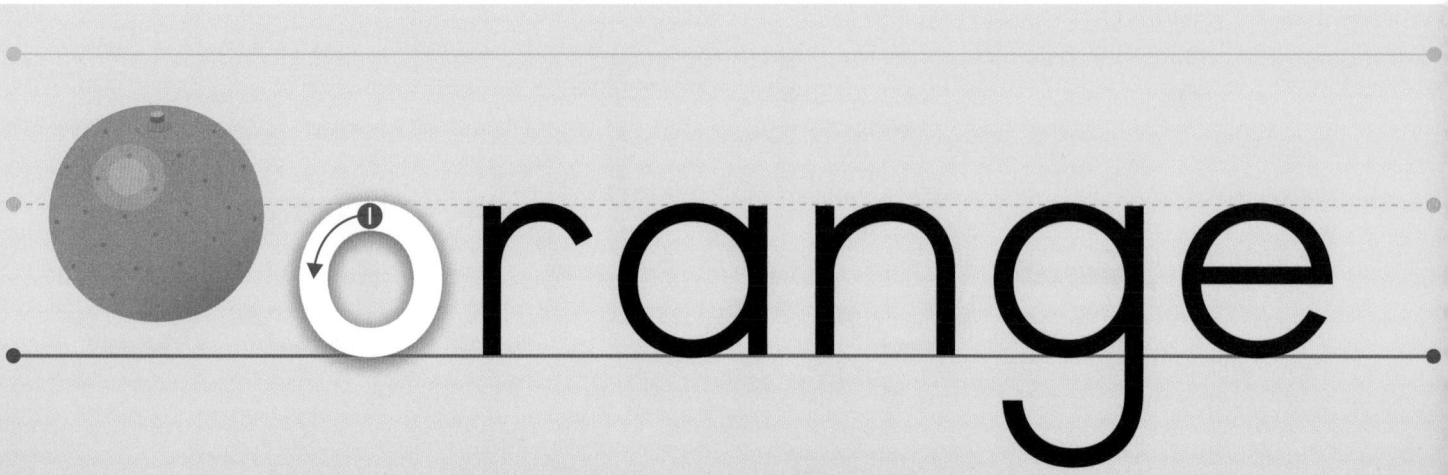

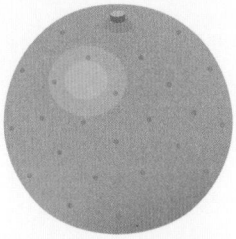

orange

octopus

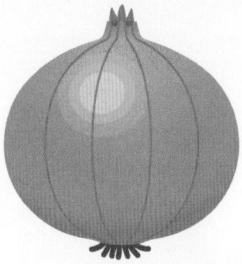

onion

owl

octopus

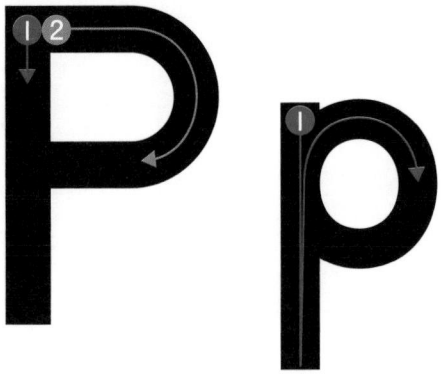

To Parents: The letter P is exactly like the first two strokes of the letter B—say, "straight line down, loop to the middle."

panda
pig
penguin
pear
panda

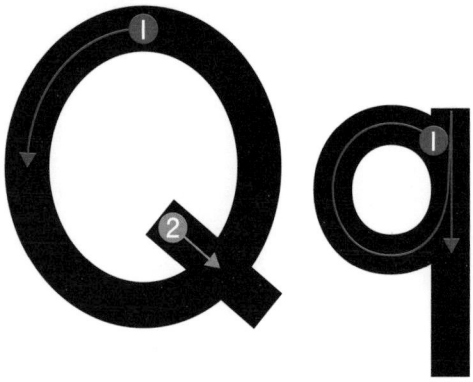

To Parents: Encourage your child to see if they can find another letter hiding inside the Q. It's the letter O. Make uppercase letter Q by starting with an O. Then draw a line that crosses through the bottom of the O.

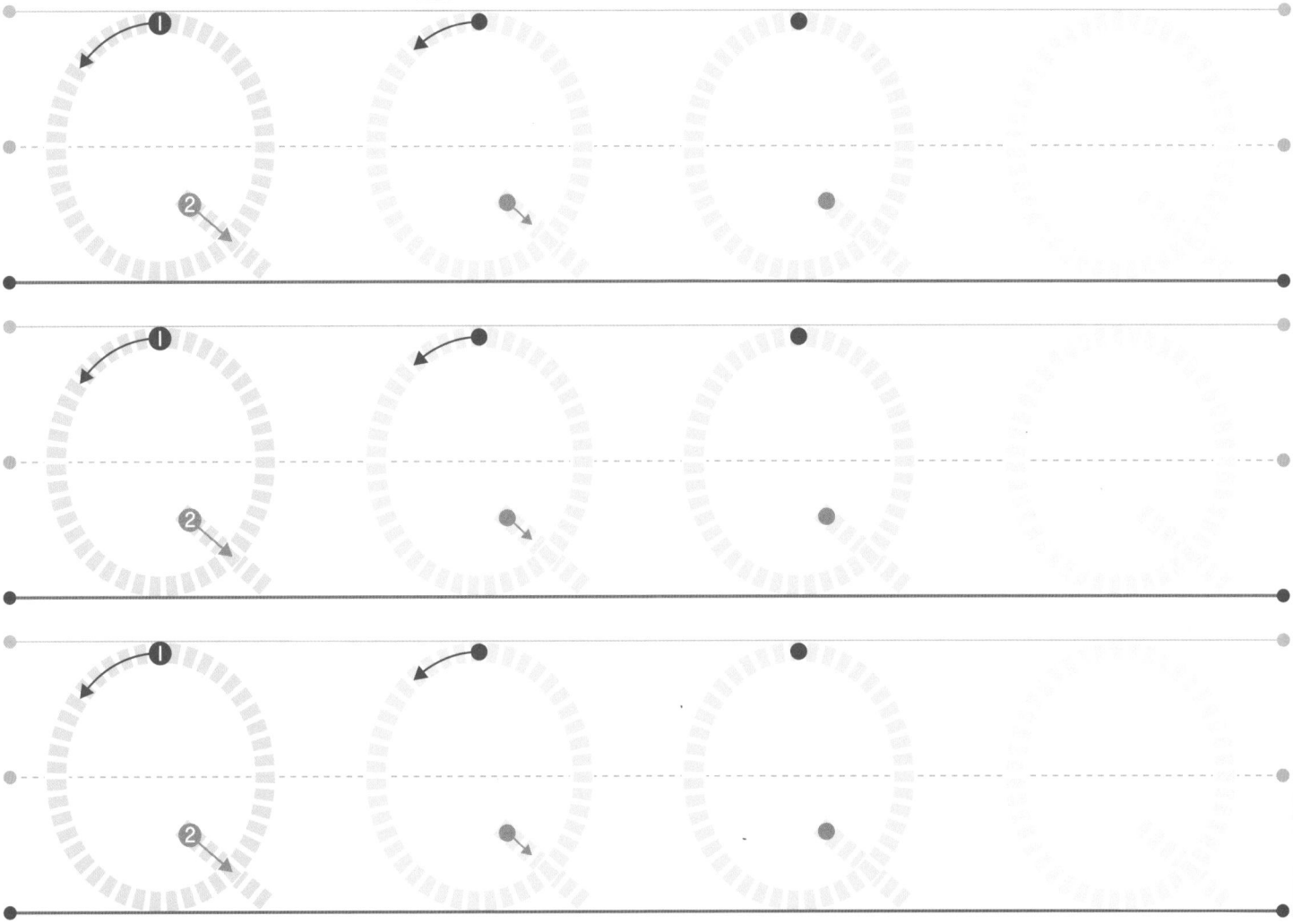

queen

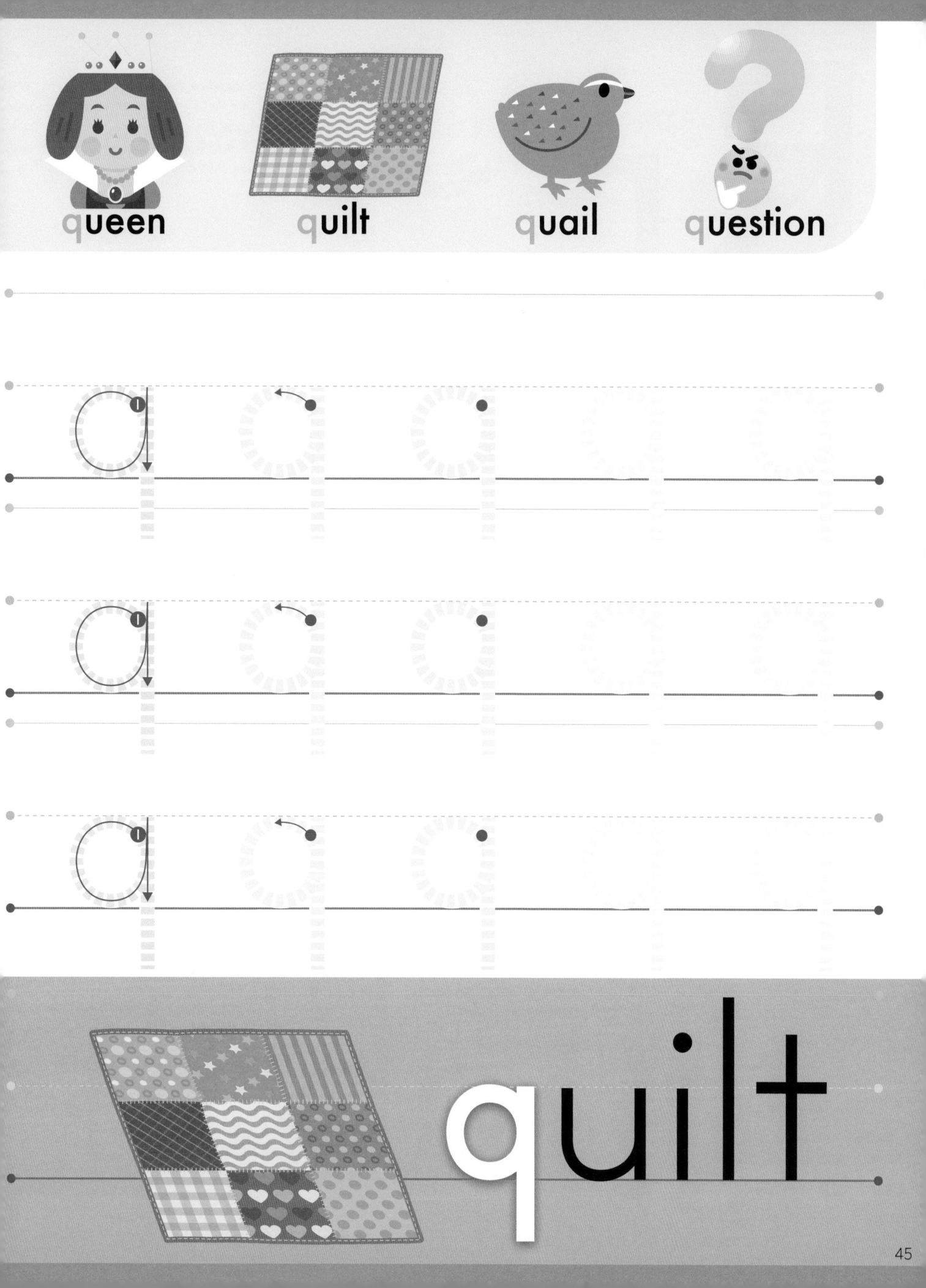
queen
quilt
quail
question
quilt

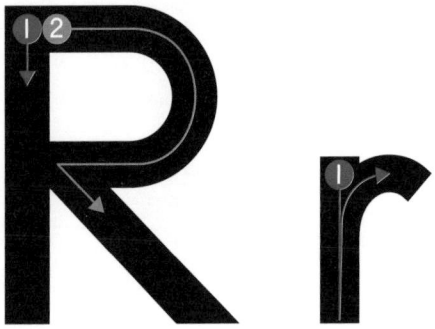

To Parents: Uppercase letter R begins the same way as uppercase B and P—say, "straight line down, loop to the middle, diagonal line to the bottom." Show them that uppercase R is the same as uppercase P except for it also has a leg that kicks out like a rabbit's foot.

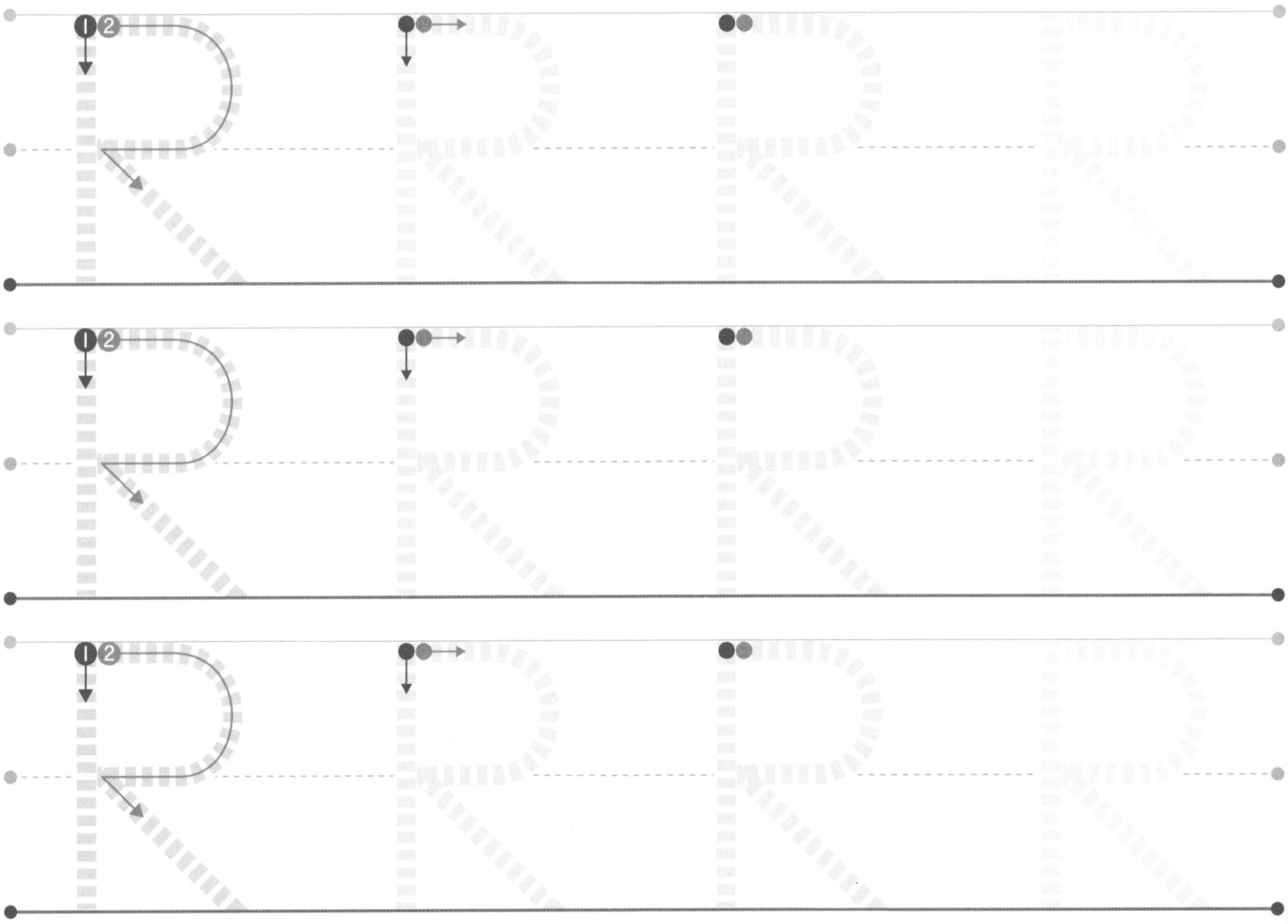

rose
rainbow
rabbit
rocket

rose

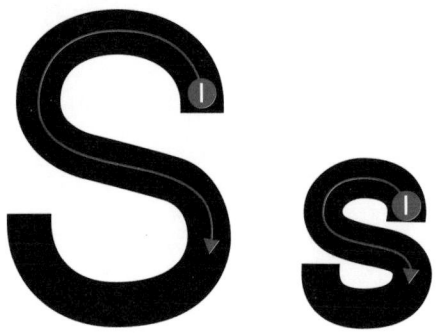

To Parents: Help your child see that some letters resemble other objects. For example, S looks like a slithering snake! Encourage your child to find the hidden letter C at the top of the S. This will help ensure that they do not reverse the direction of the S.

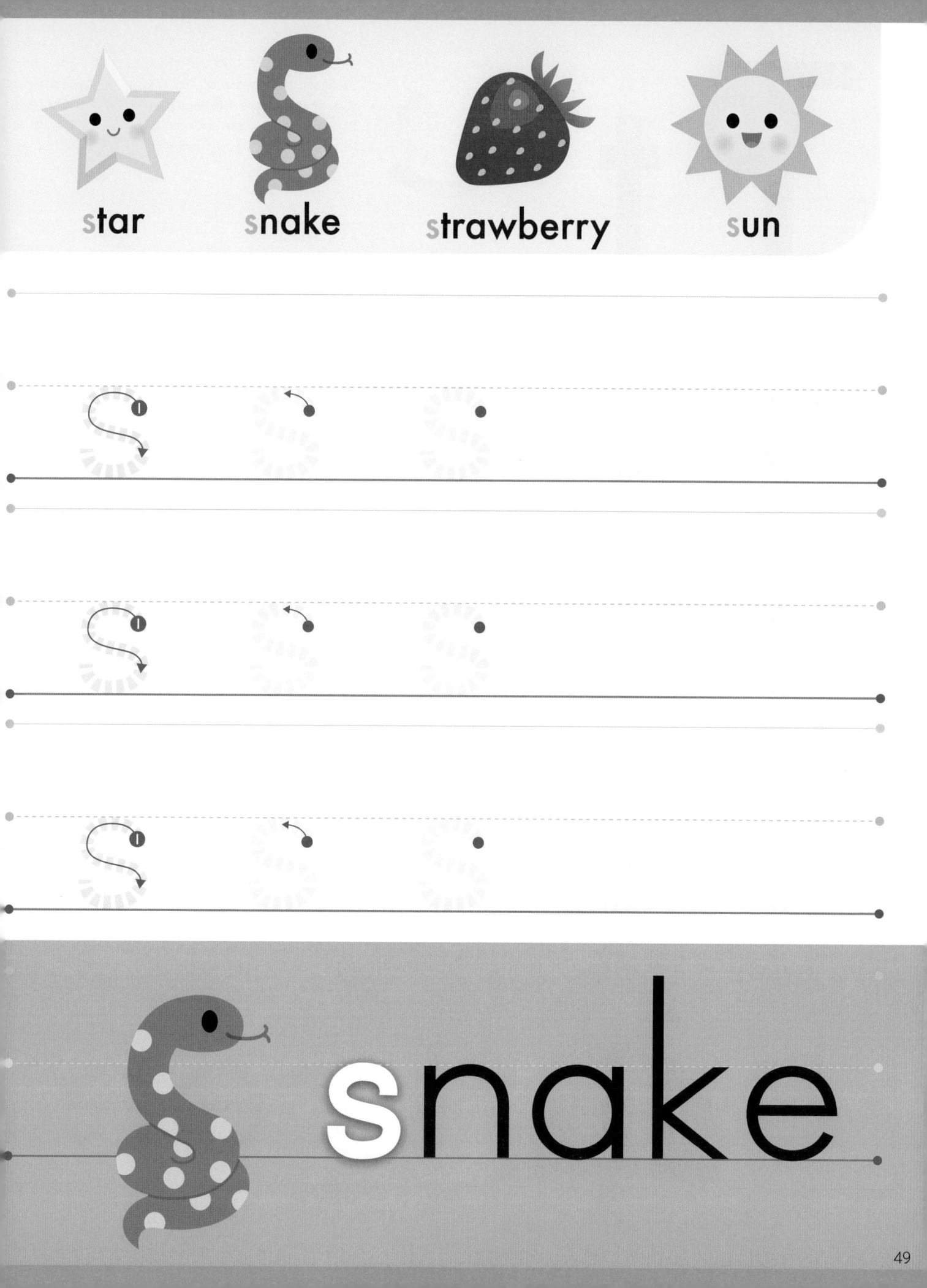
star
snake
strawberry
sun
snake

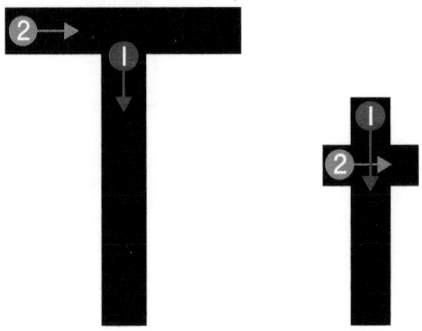

To Parents: Uppercase letter T is made the exact same way as uppercase I except it does not have the line at the bottom. Help your child notice the ways that letters are similar and different from one another.

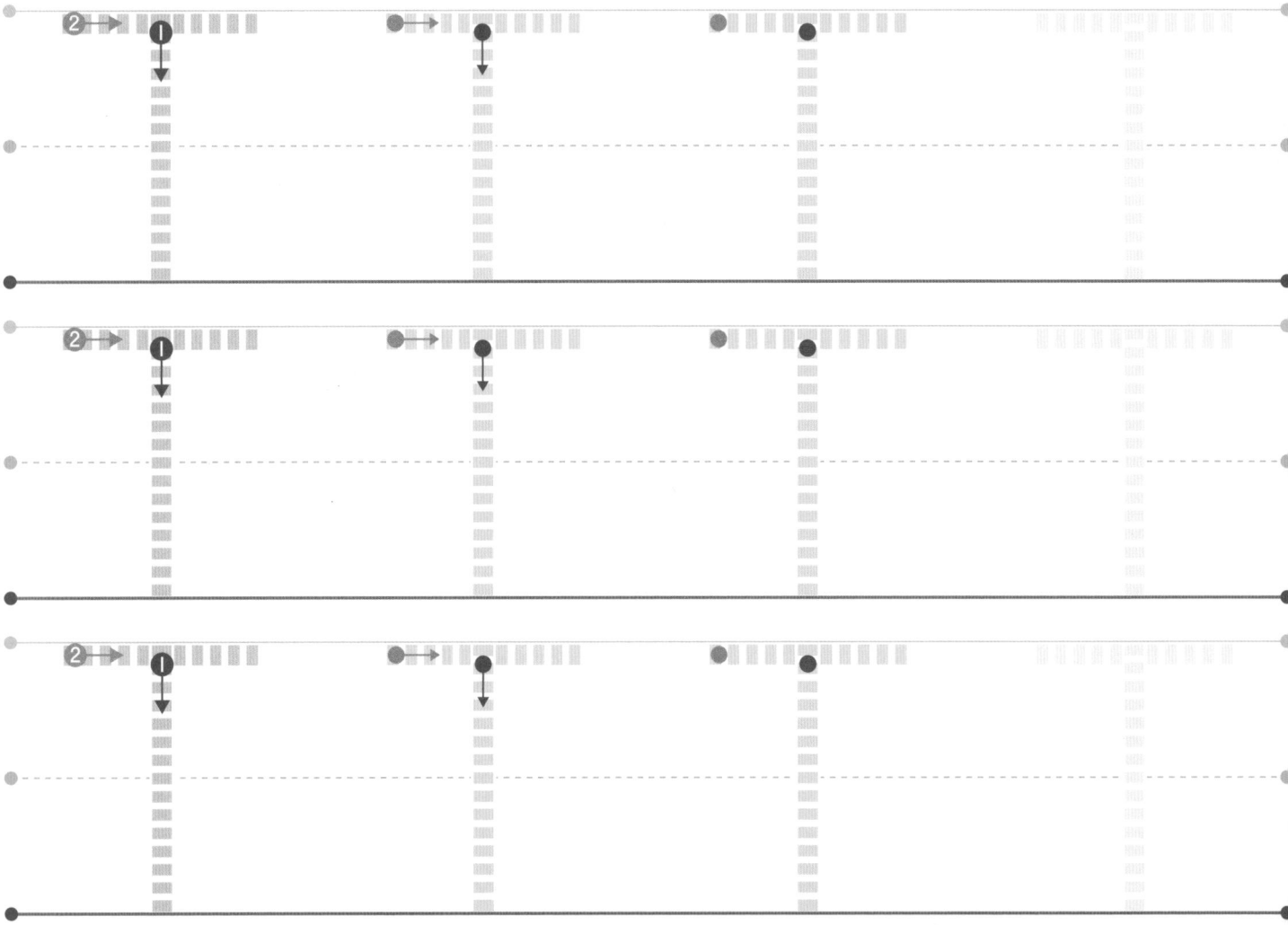

tiger
tree
turtle
tomato

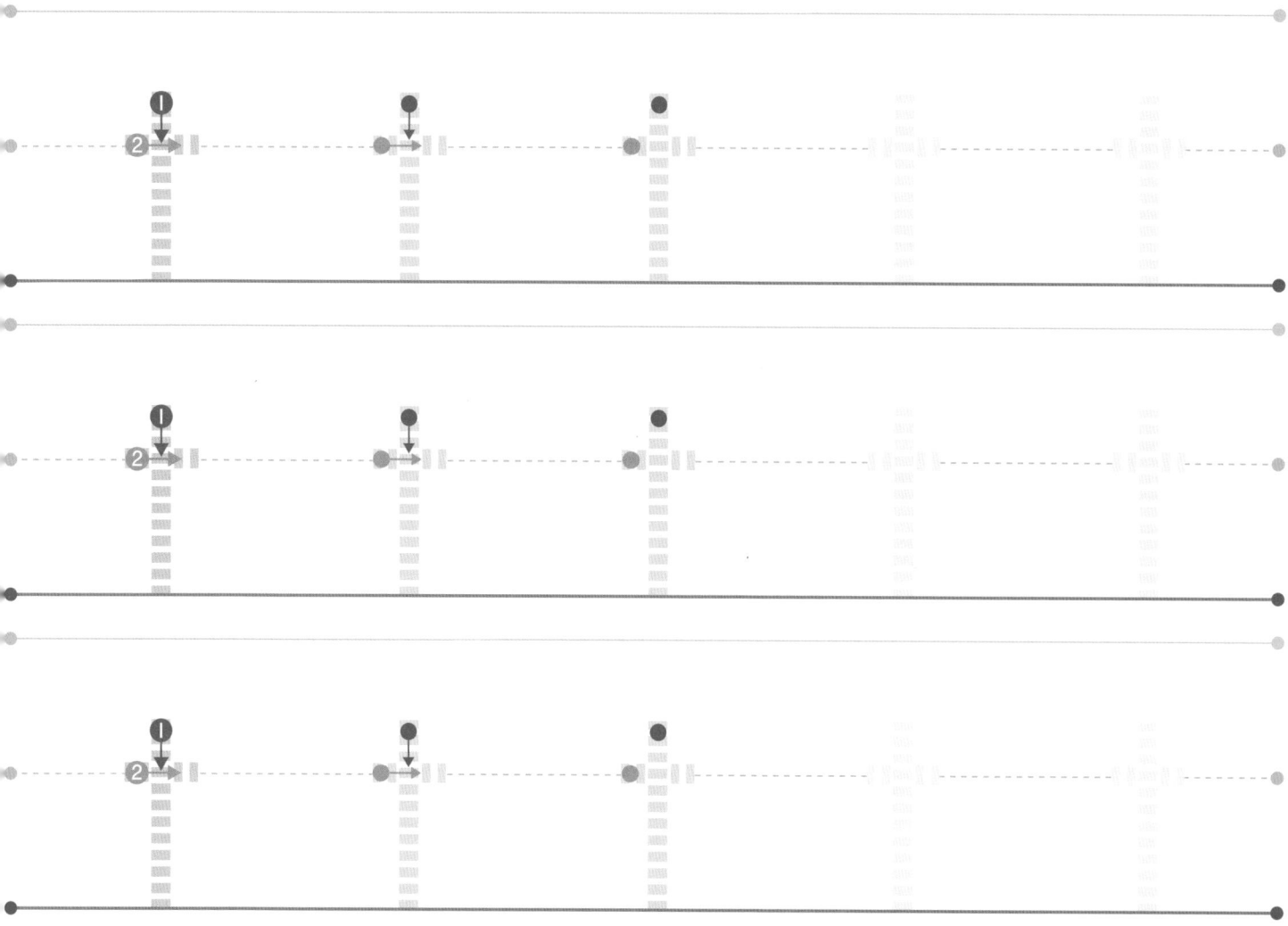
1
2
1
2
1
2

tomato

U u

To Parents: To keep it fun and interesting, play Simon Says: Writing Edition. You might say, "Simon Says find the letter U page and write four Us all by yourself." Making it into a game will help your child develop a positive association with writing.

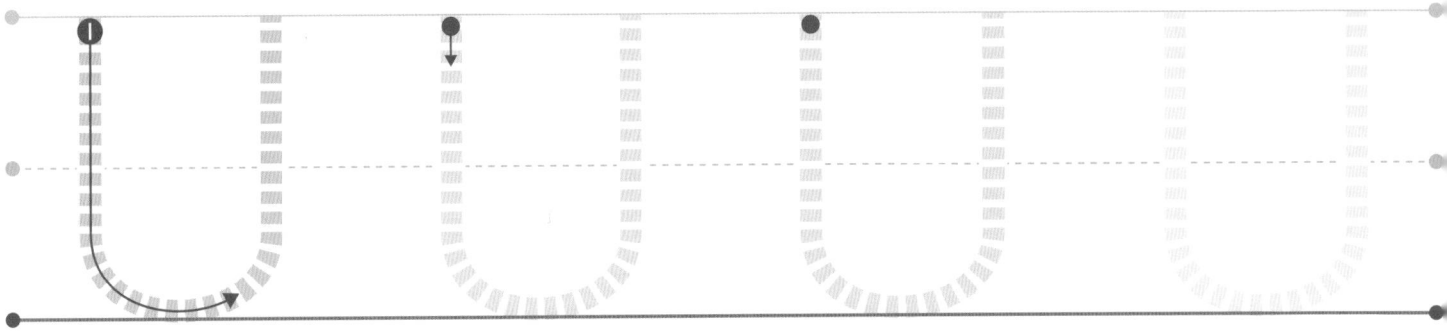

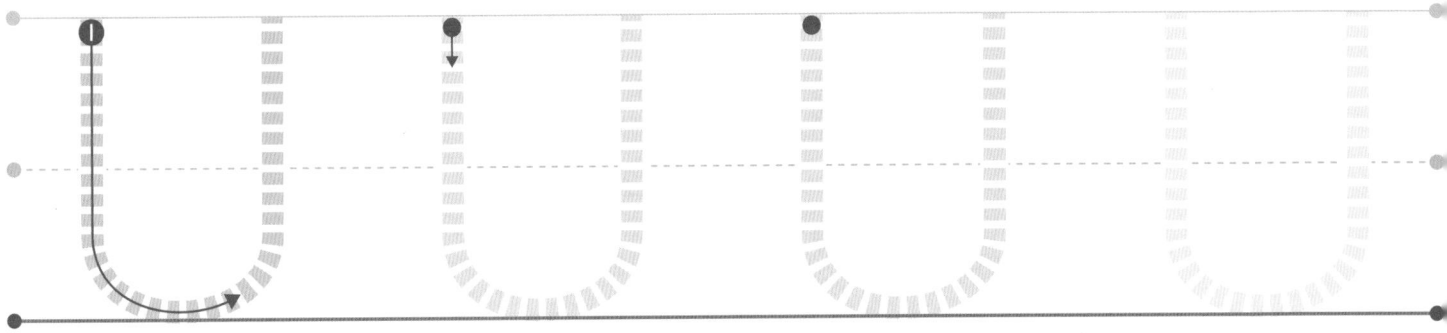

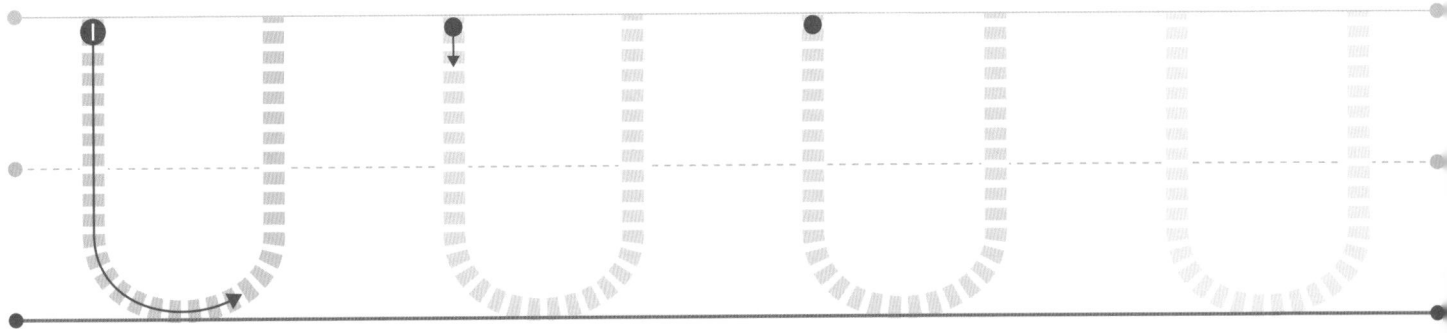

underwear
umbrella
UFO
unicorn

umbrella

V v

To Parents: Teach the letters V and W the same day. Once your child has mastered V, move on to W.

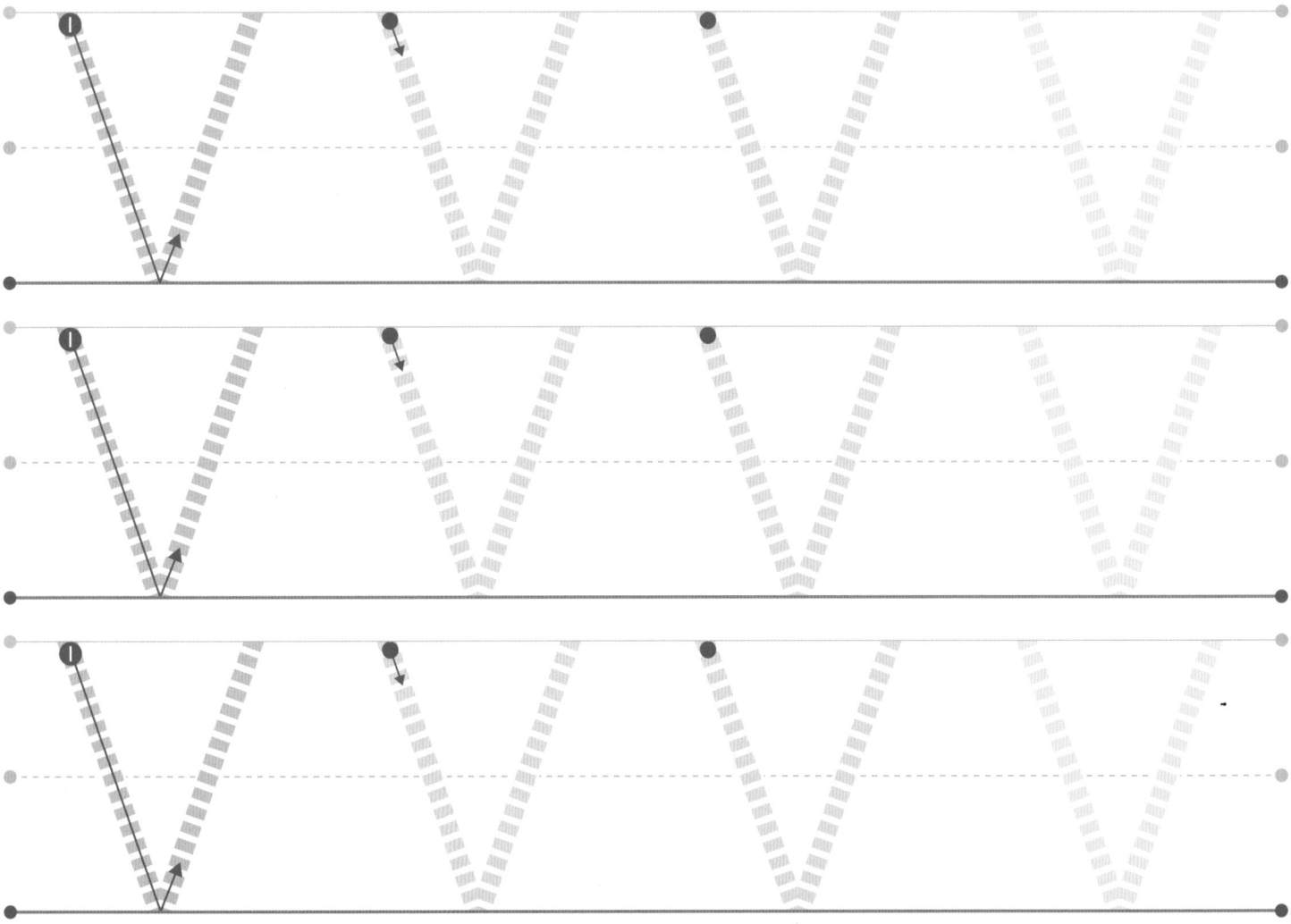

violin

vegetables
vacuum
violin
van

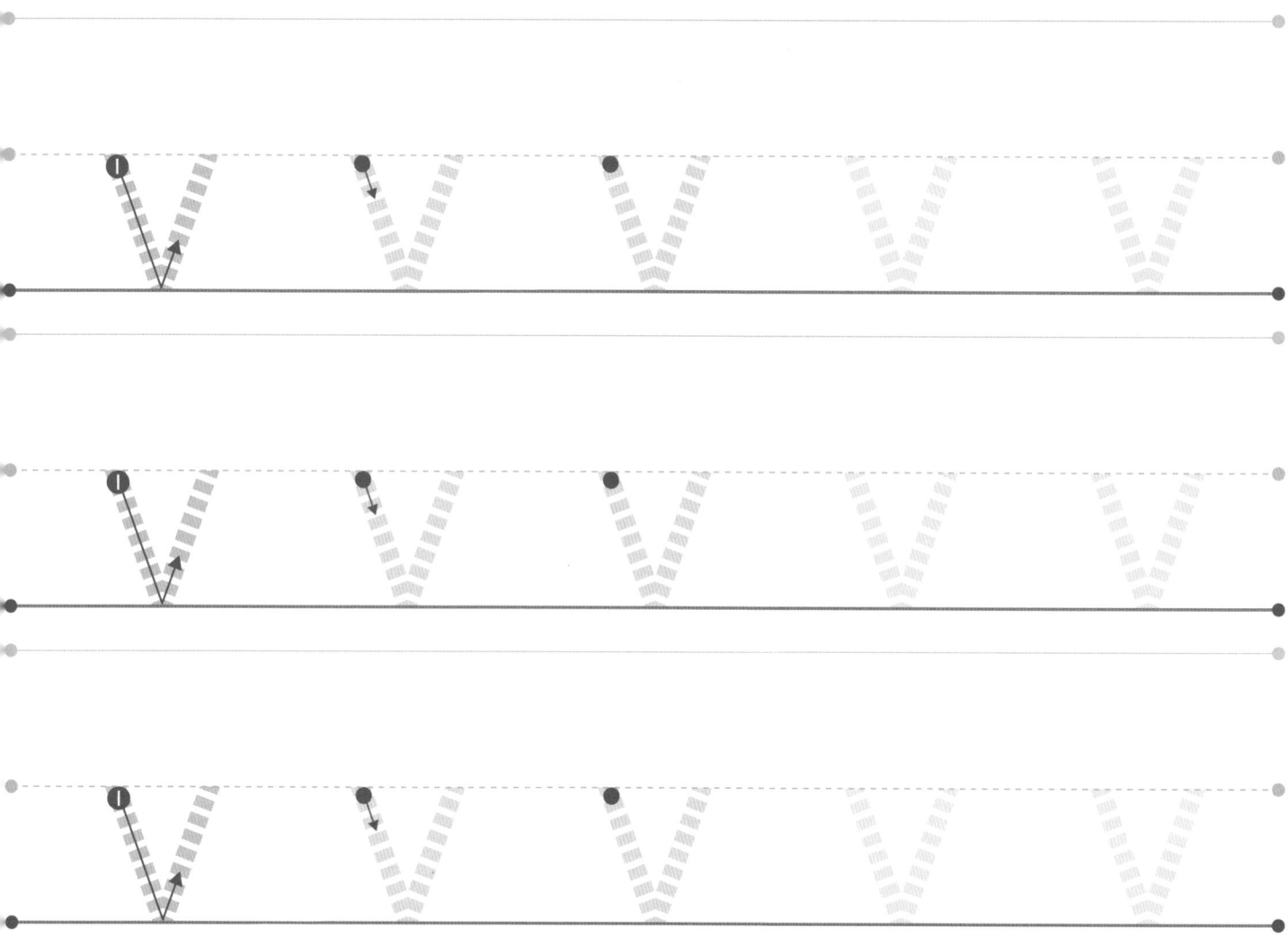

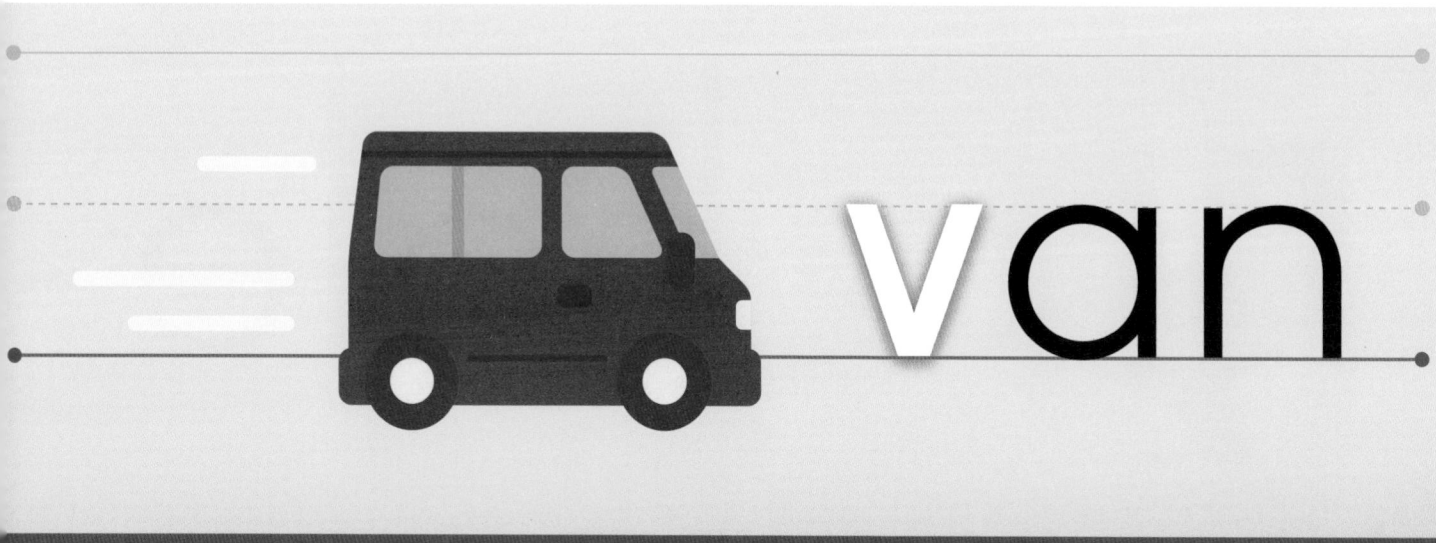
van

Ww

To Parents: The letter W is like two Vs stuck together. Make one V and then continue down with another diagonal line. Then come back up.

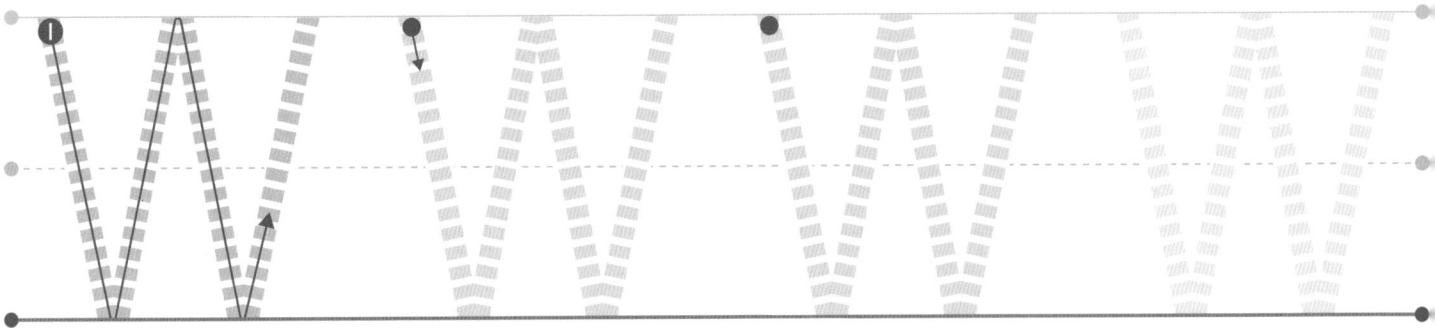

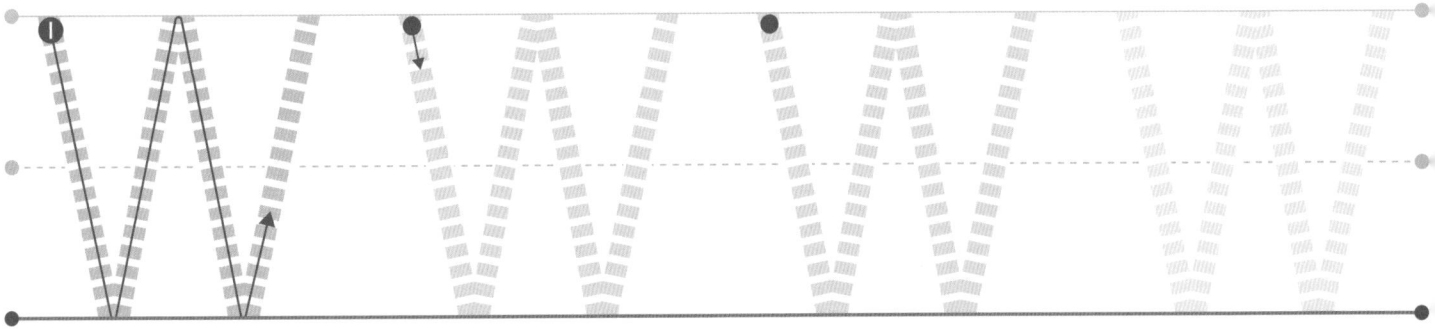

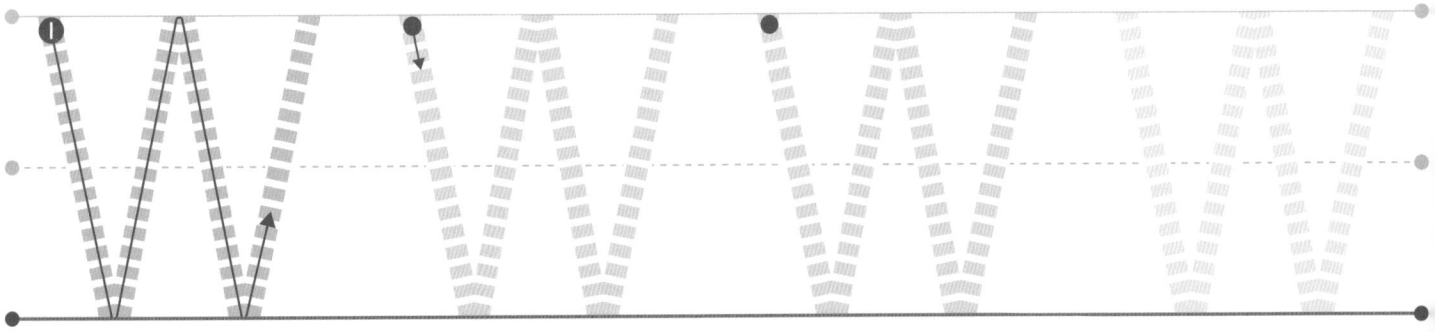

whale
watermelon
wolf
window

wolf

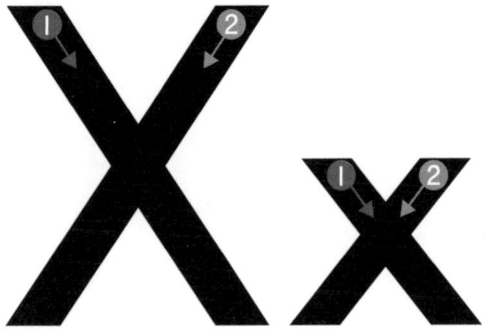

To Parents: As your child becomes more confident with letter writing, allow them to teach a younger sibling or stuffed animal the proper letter formation. Research shows that teaching is a great way to commit information to memory.

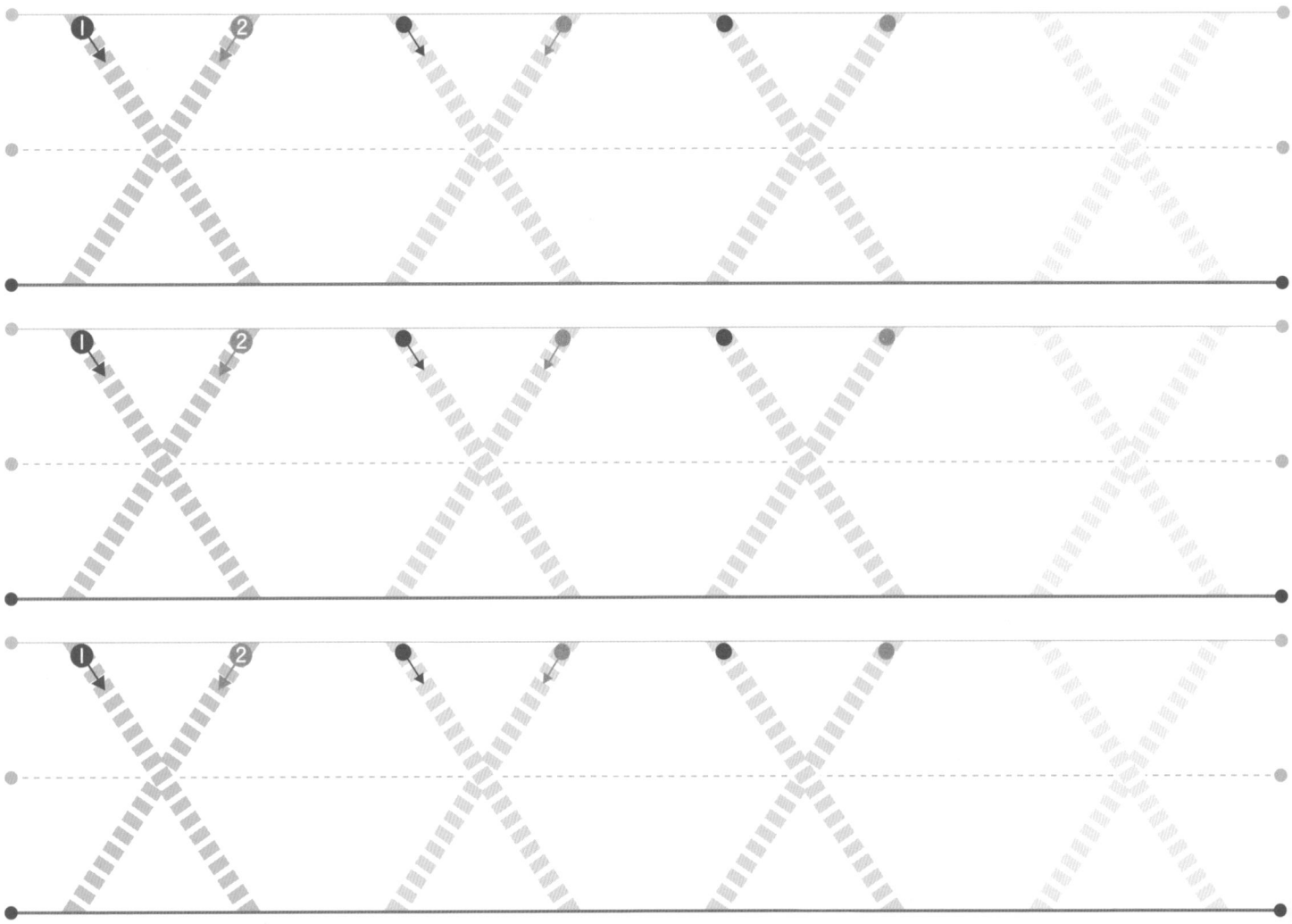

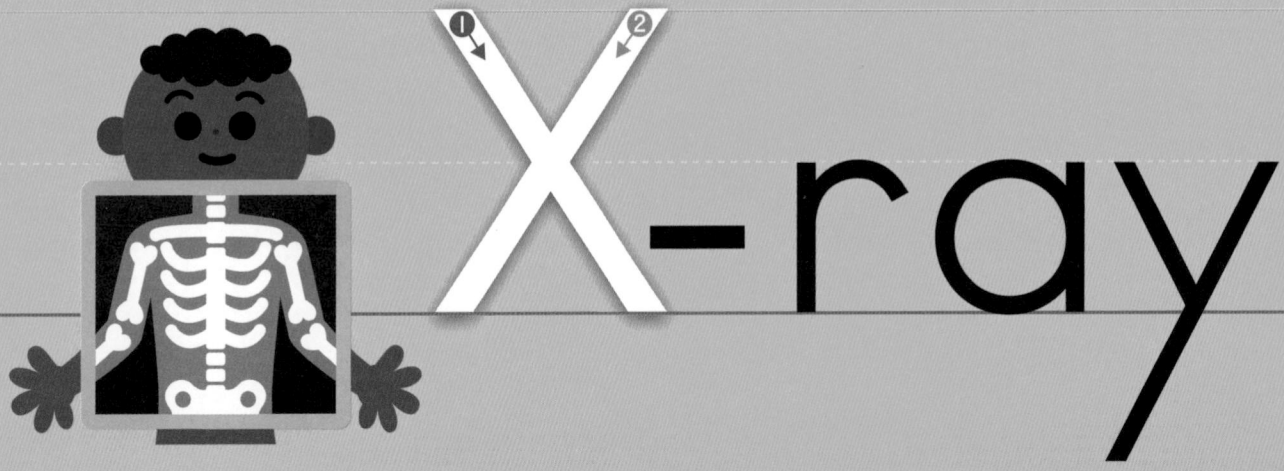

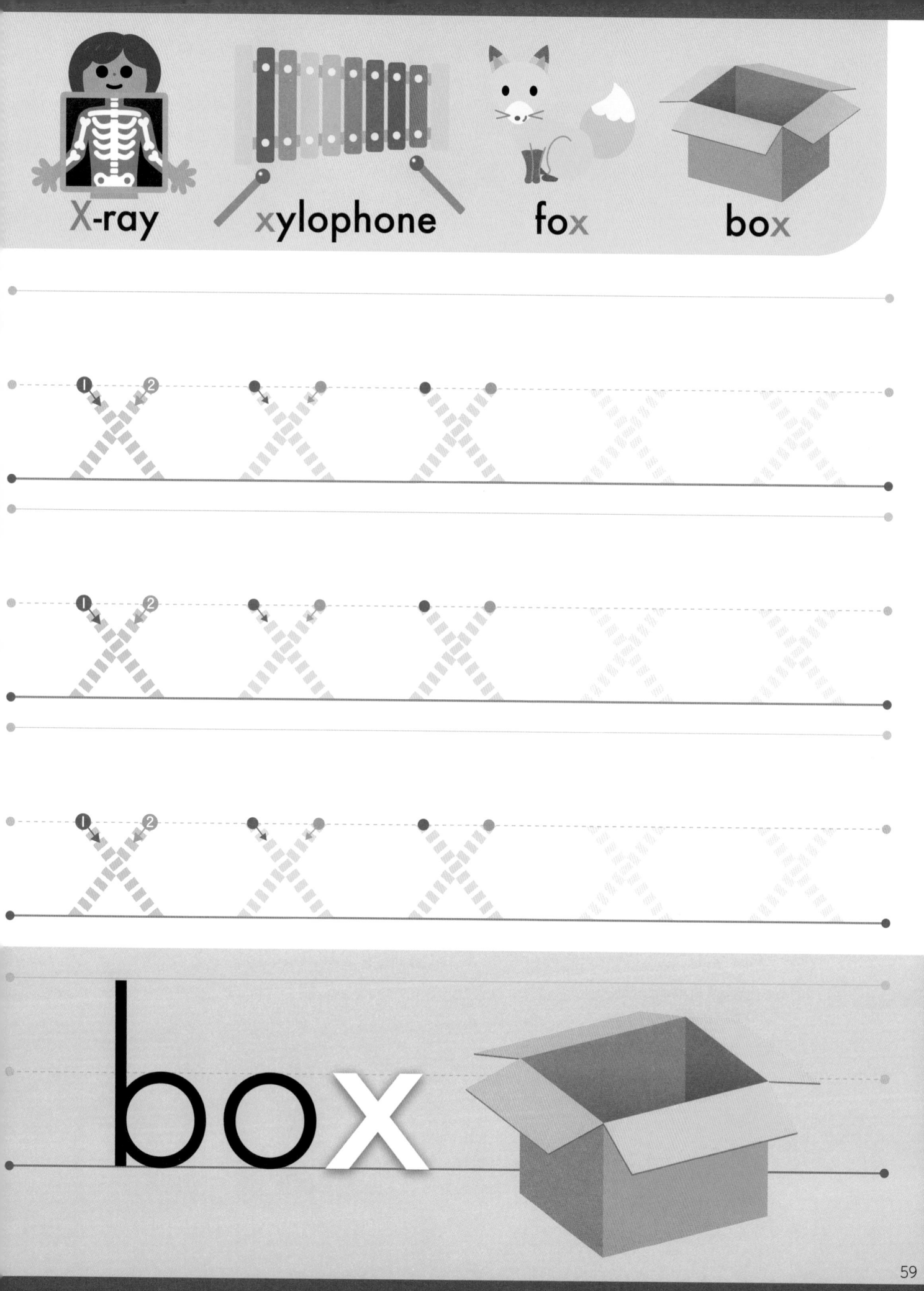
X-ray
xylophone
fox
box
box

Yy

To Parents: Have your child notice that the second diagonal line meets the first diagonal line in the middle. Stop where they meet and draw a line all the way down.

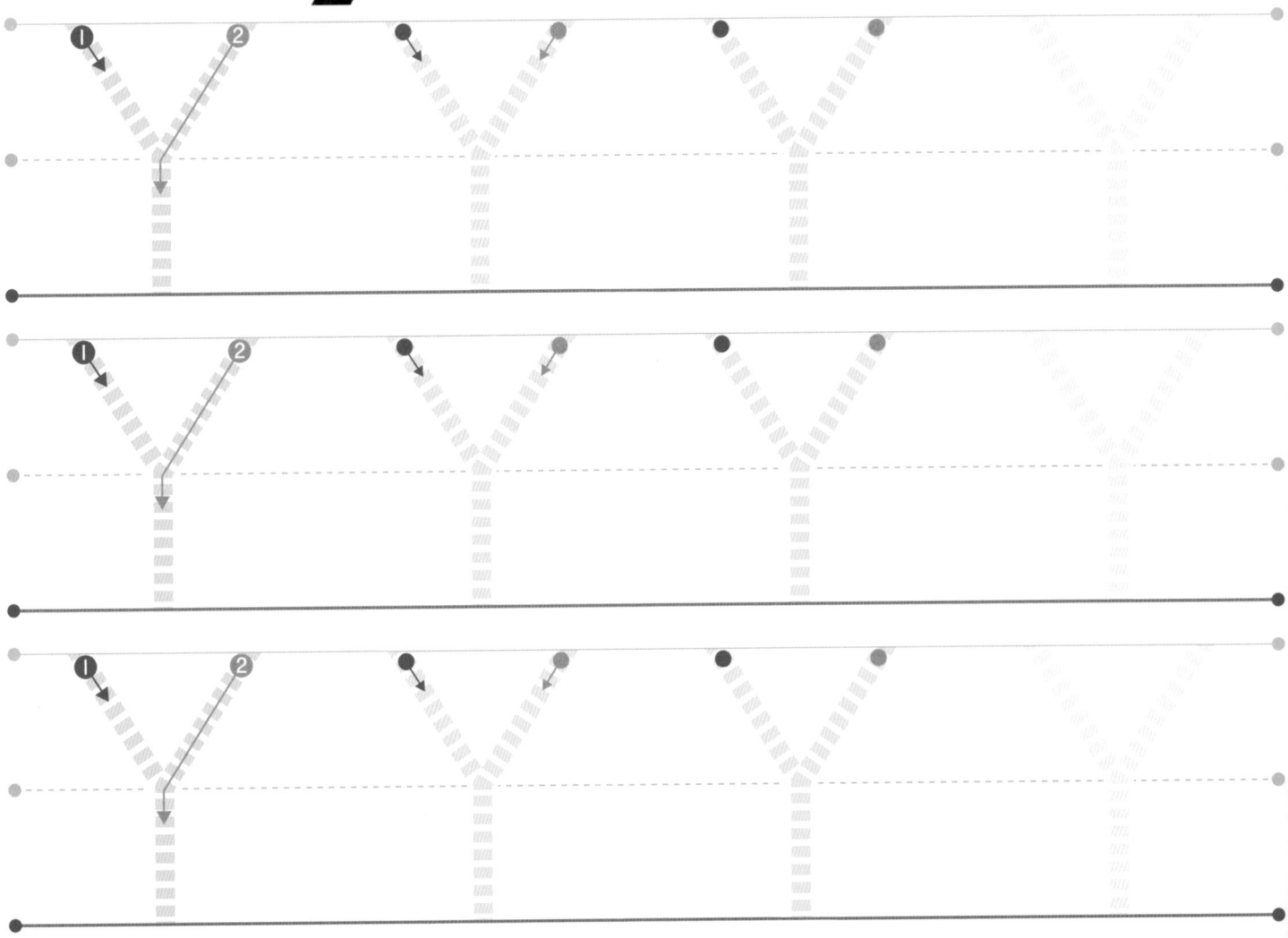

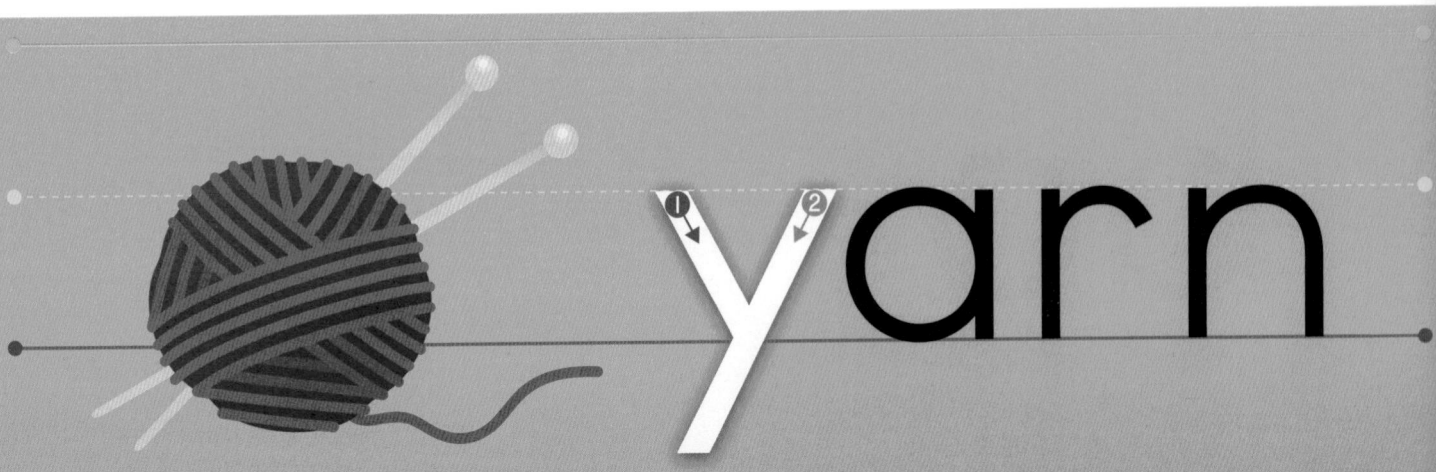

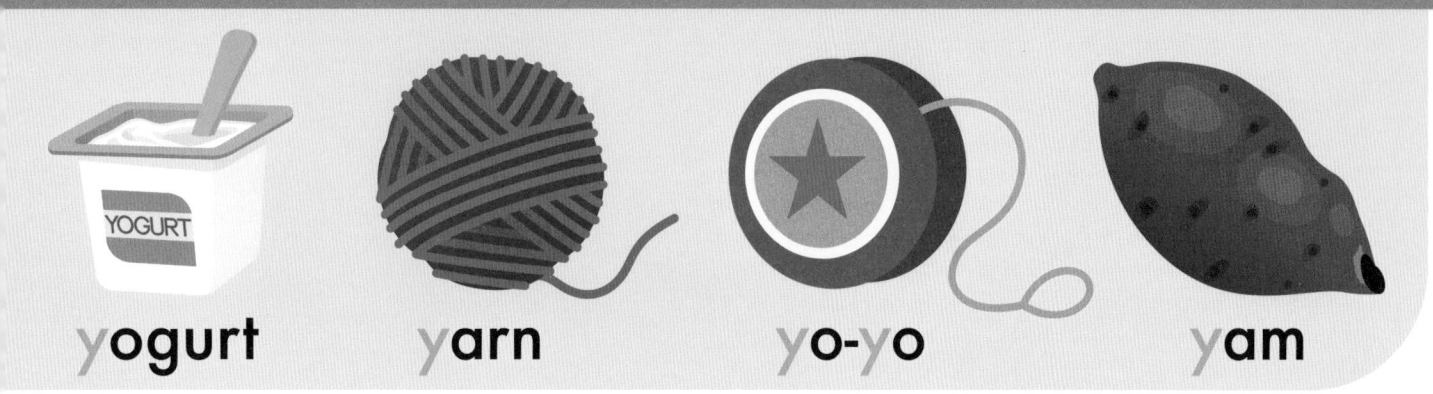
YOGURT
yogurt
yarn
yo-yo
yam

YOGURT
yogurt

Z z

To Parents: Children often confuse the letters S and Z as they look similar. However, the two letters face opposite directions. It is helpful to remind your child that Z is a very similar shape to the number 2. It starts with a line across, then a connected diagonal line, and then another line across.

zebra

zoo

zebra

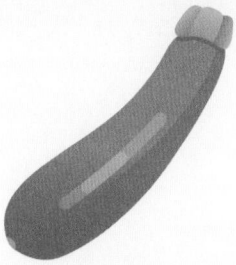

zucchini

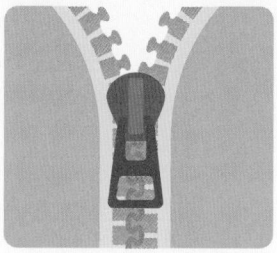

zipper

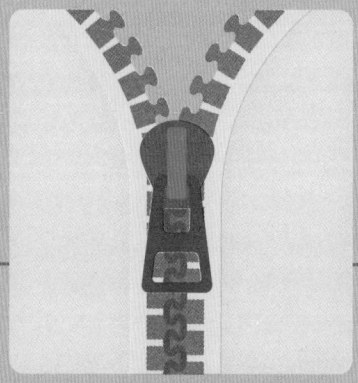

zipper

Trace the letters again from A to Z. Say the word below each letter.

Aa Bb Cc

apple bear cat

Dd Ee Ff

dog elephant fish

Gg Hh Ii

giraffe hat ice cream

Jj Kk Ll

jet koala lion

Mm Nn Oo

monkey necklace octopus

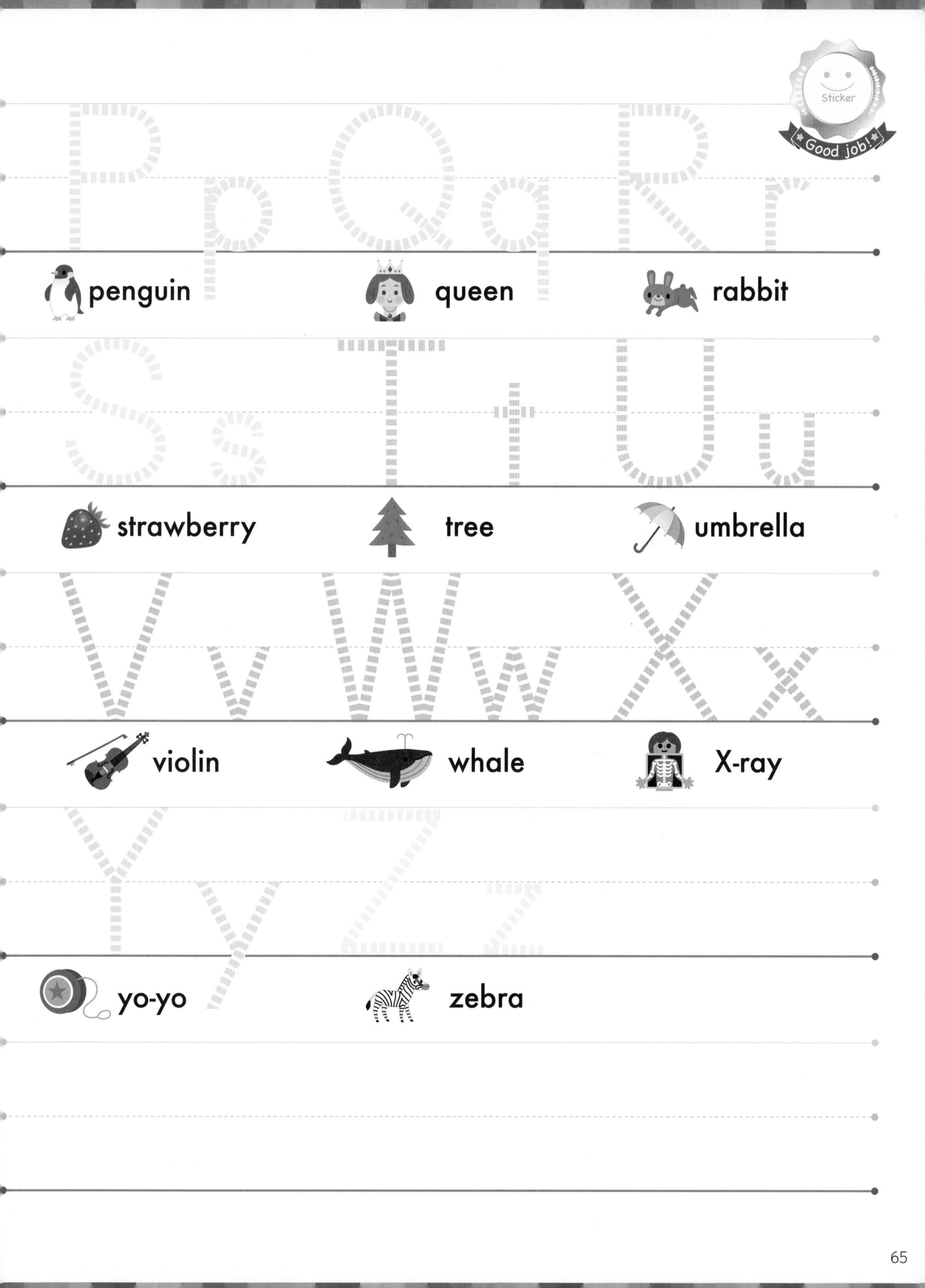
Sticker
Good job!
Pp Qq Rr
penguin
queen
rabbit
Ss Tt Uu
strawberry
tree
umbrella
Vv Ww Xx
violin
whale
X-ray
Yy Zz
yo-yo
zebra

Numbers Trace the numbers.

To Parents: Encourage your child to trace with a crayon or pencil. If they have difficulty using the crayon independently, have them trace with their finger first.

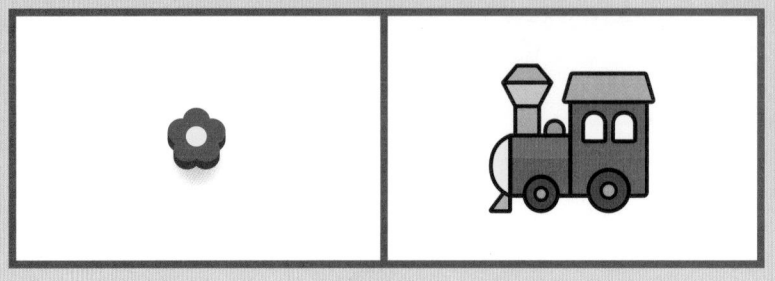

Sticker

Good job!

one

Write the number and the word. Then, count the objects.

one

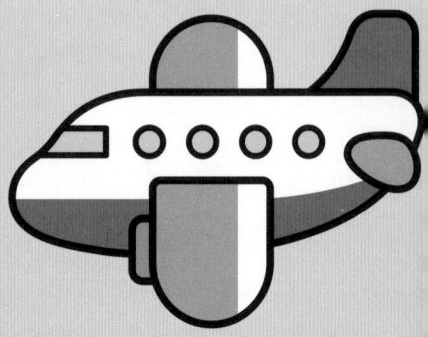

2

To Parents: After drawing a curve, have your child stop the pencil once and draw a horizontal line.

two

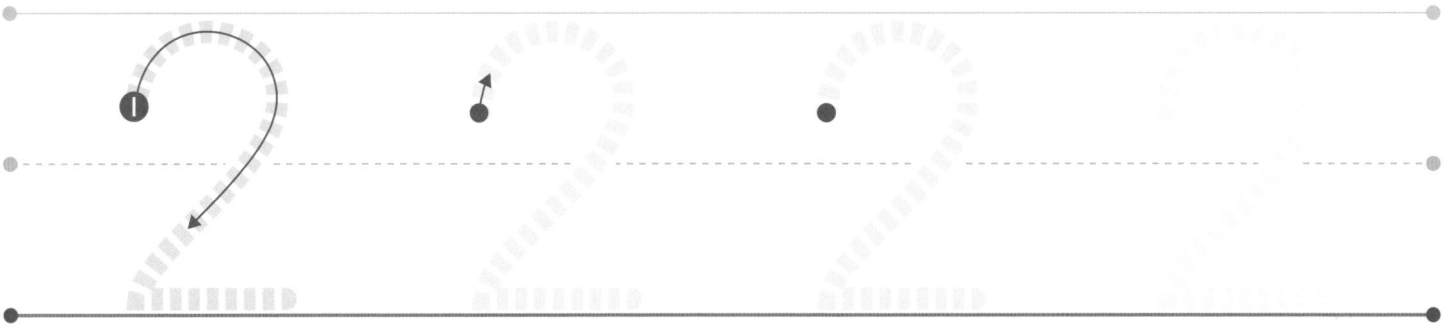

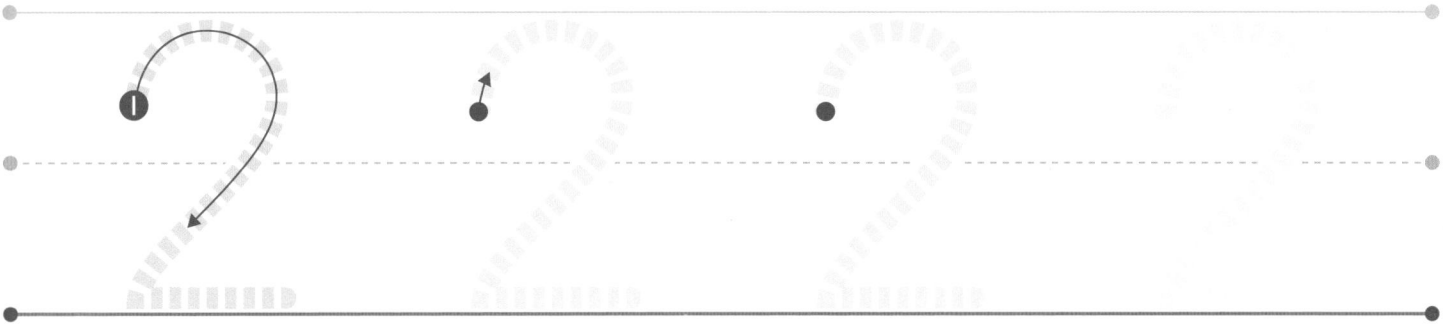

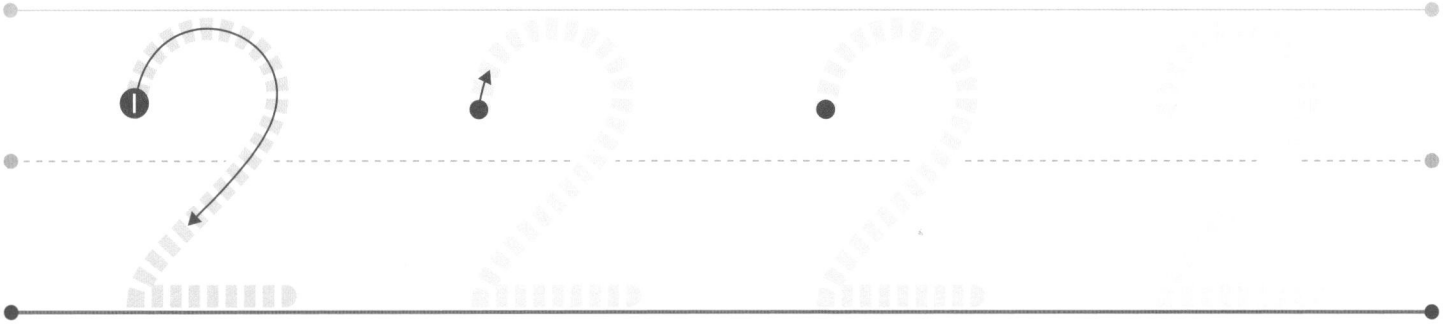

3

To Parents: Show your child the three flowers on the page. Emphasize that the number 3 represents three objects—in this case, three flowers.

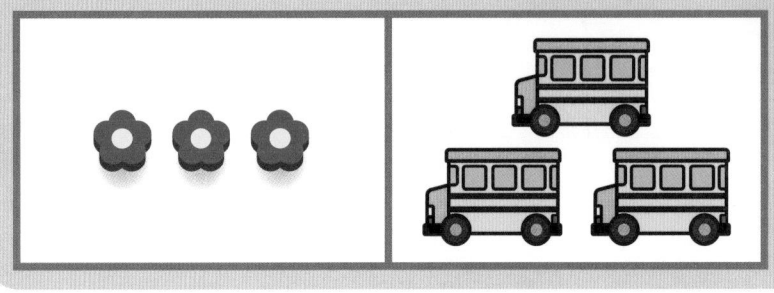

Sticker

Good job!

three

Write the number and the word. Then, count the objects.

3 three

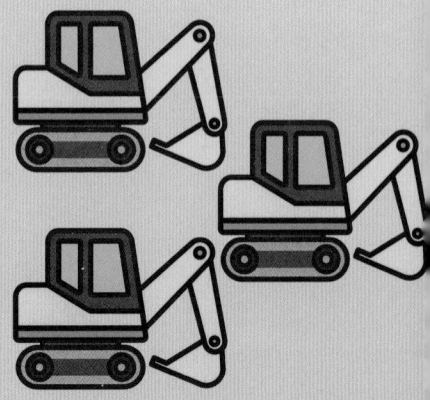

4

To Parents: To write the number 4, your child will use two pencil strokes. The sample below has numbered lines that show your child the order in which they should make the strokes.

four

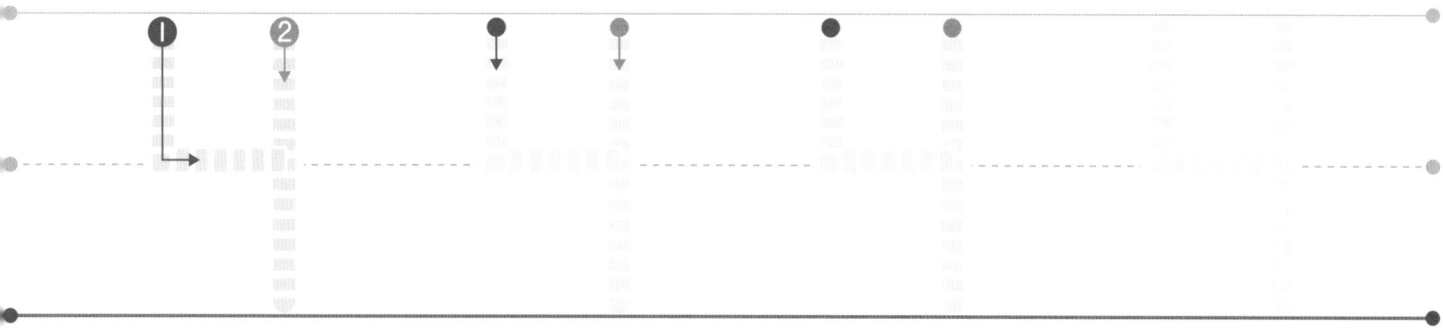

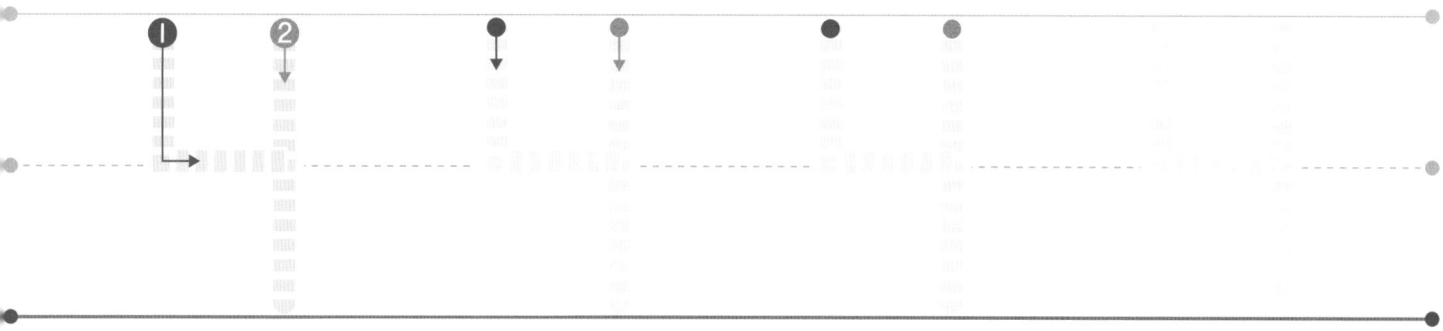

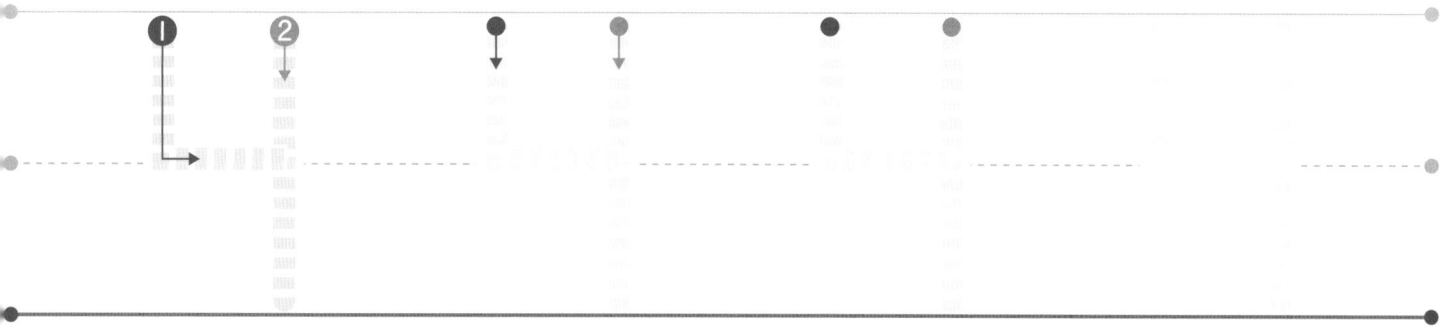

5

To Parents: The number 5 requires drawing two separate lines. Demonstrate how to draw with your finger first. Then, encourage your child to try.

five

Write the number and the word. Then, count the objects.

5 five

6

To Parents: If your child has difficulty writing the number 6, practice drawing the spirals on page 10.

six

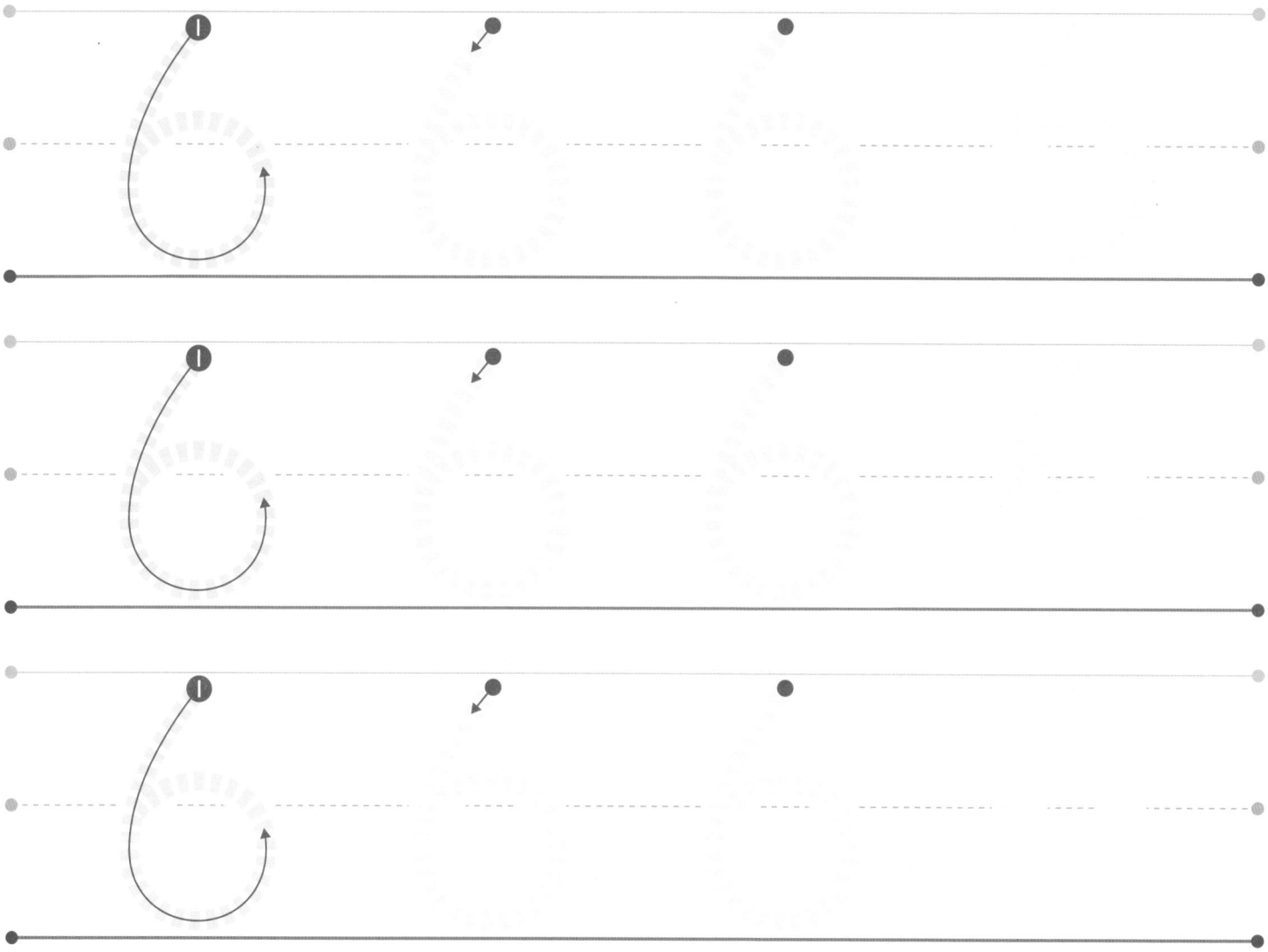

7

To Parents: Ask your child to say the number aloud as they trace it with a crayon or pencil.

seven

Write the number and the word. Then, count the objects.

7 seven

8

To Parents: When a child counts several objects, they may lose track. Your child can color, circle, or draw a line through the objects in order to visually recognize what has and hasn't been counted.

eight

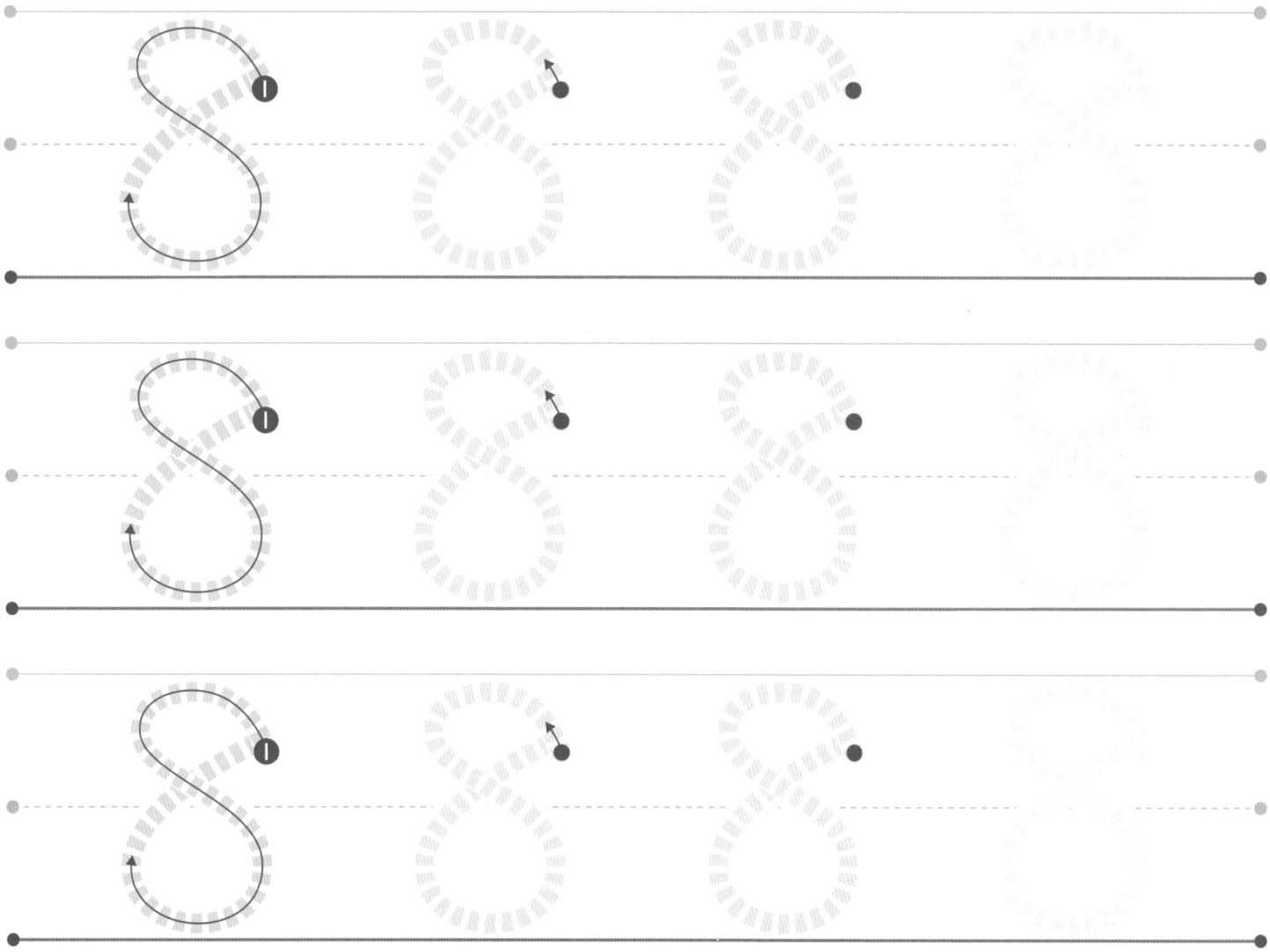

9

To Parents: When your child counts objects, make sure they point to each one with their finger. Try placing nine objects on the table and count them together.

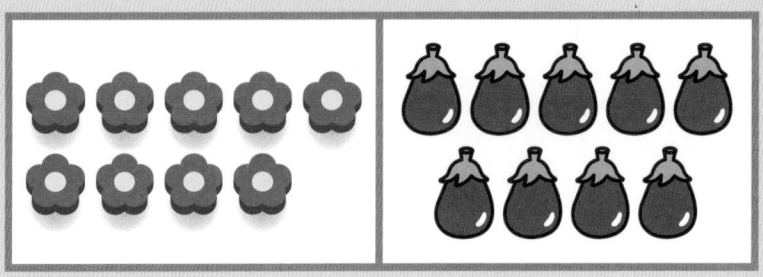

nine

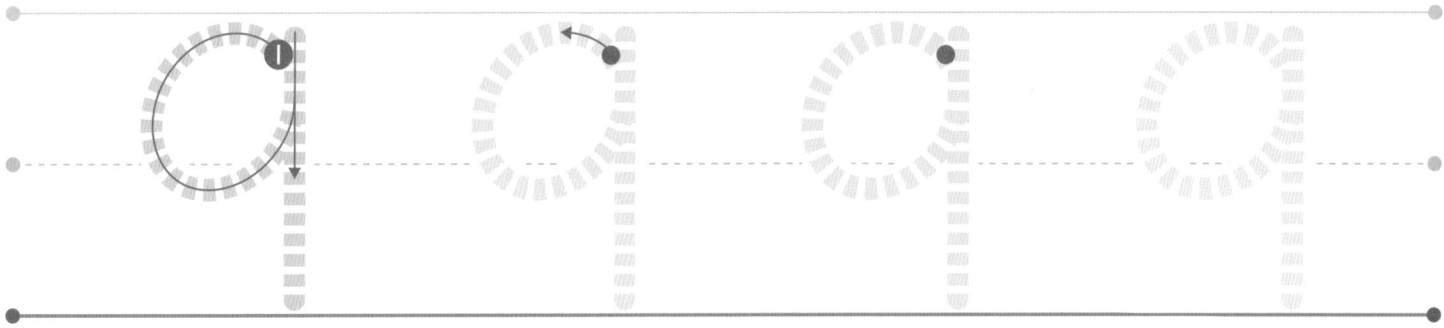

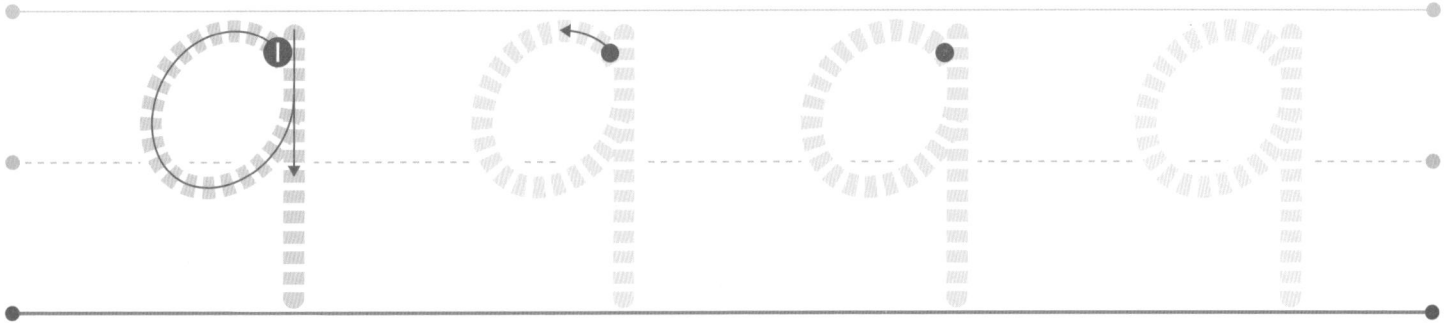

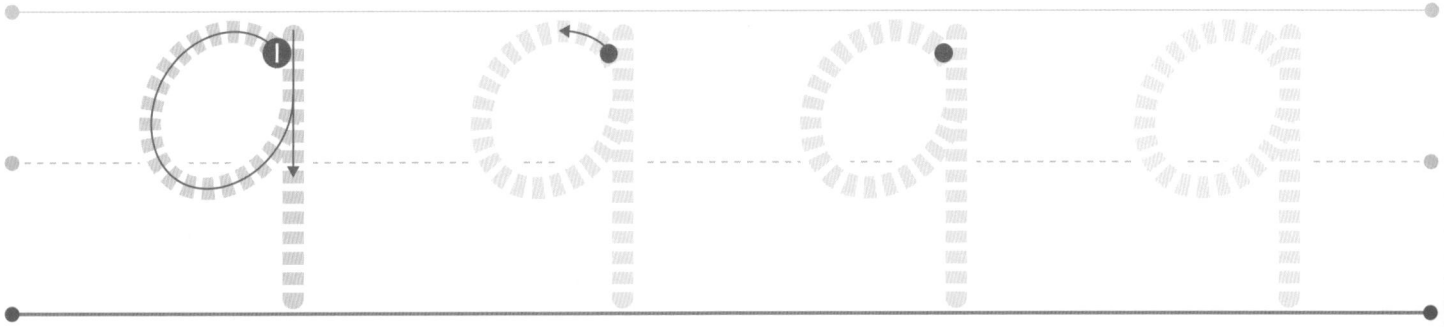

Write the number and the word. Then, count the objects.

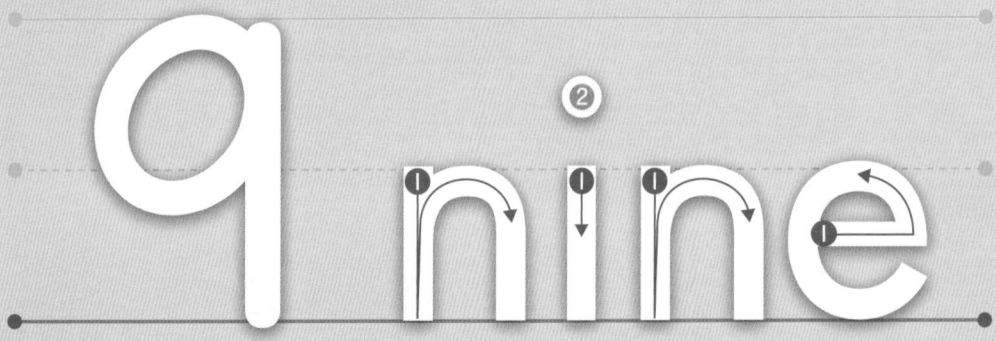

10

To Parents: If your child has difficulty writing the number 0, practice drawing the circles on page 9.

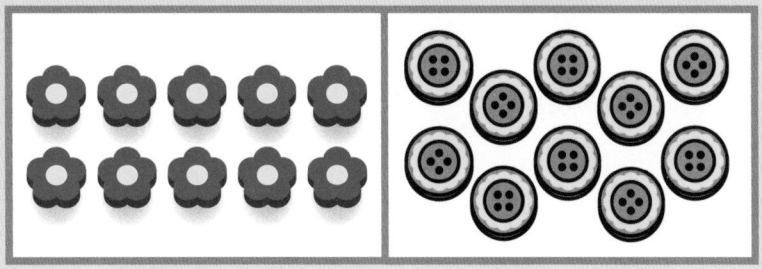

ten

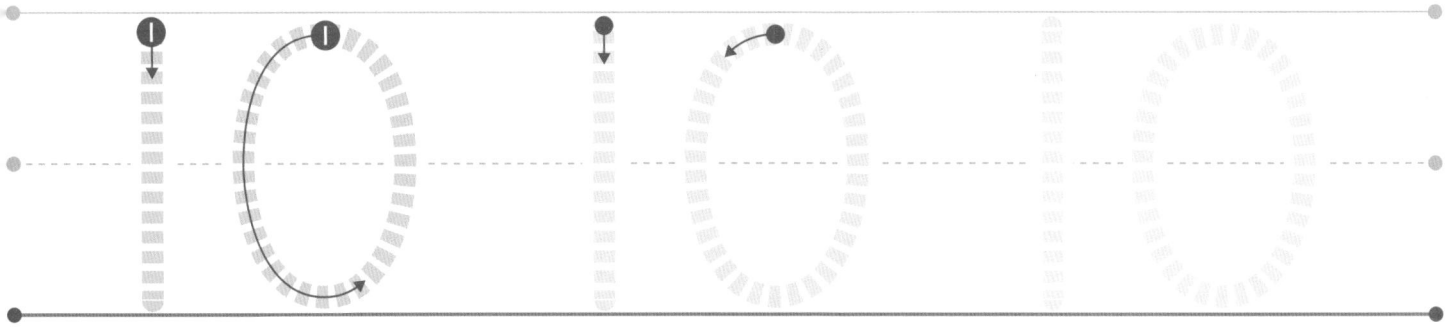

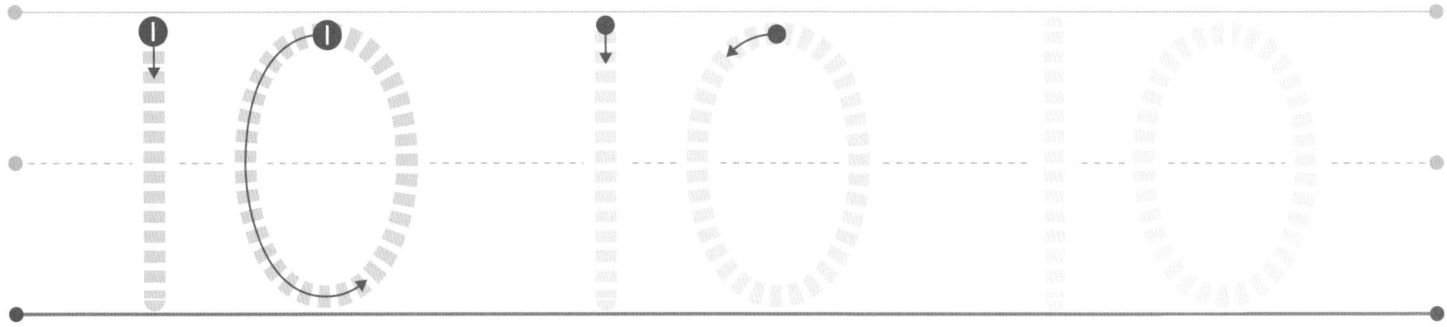

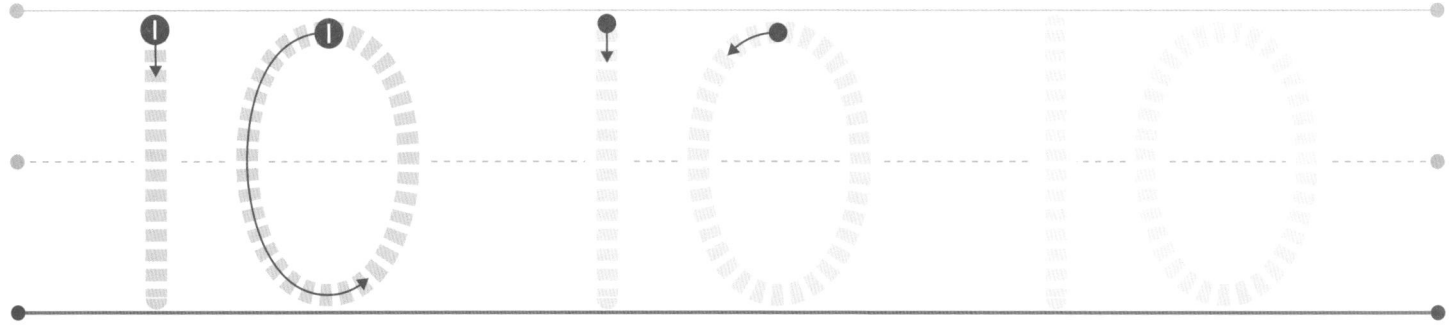

Draw a line to connect each number with the same number of flowers.
Then, connect each flower grouping with the same number of objects.

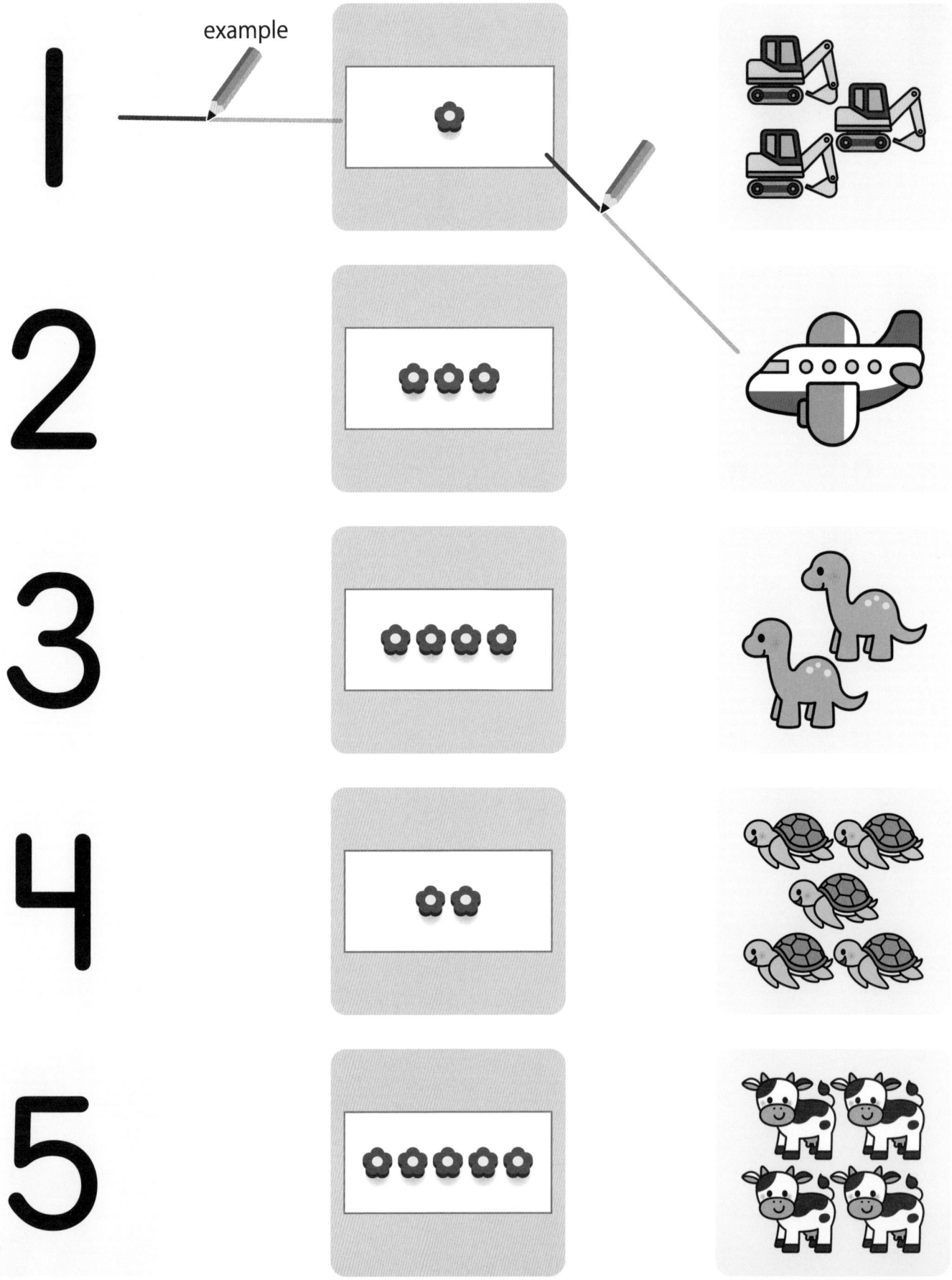

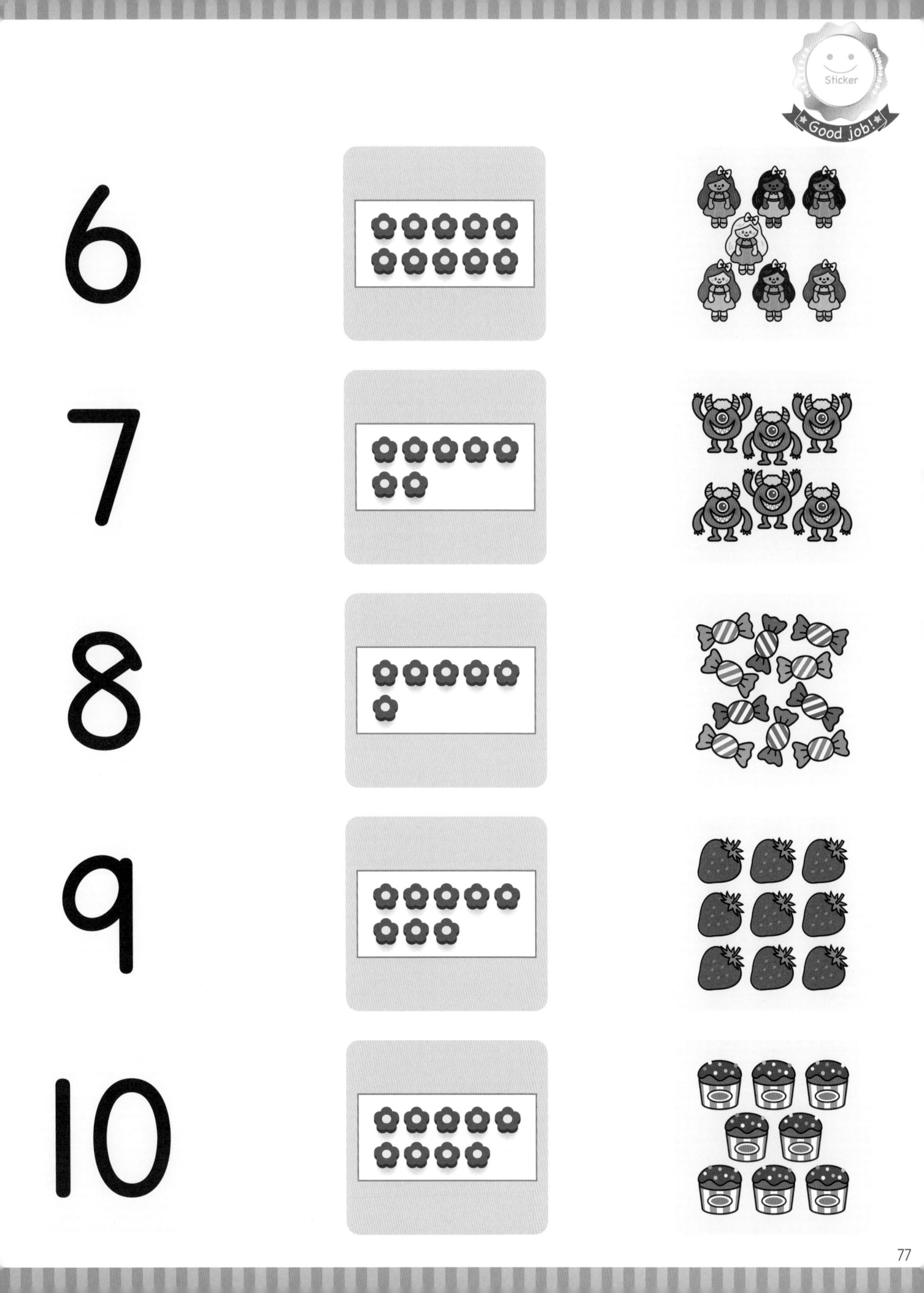
Sticker
Good job!
6
7
8
9
10

Say the numbers in order from 1 to 10, then trace the numbers below.

Sticker

Good job!

1 → 2 → 3 → 4 → 5 → 6 → 7 → 8 → 9 → 10

Draw lines from 1 to 5 in order.

Draw lines from 1 to 10 in order.

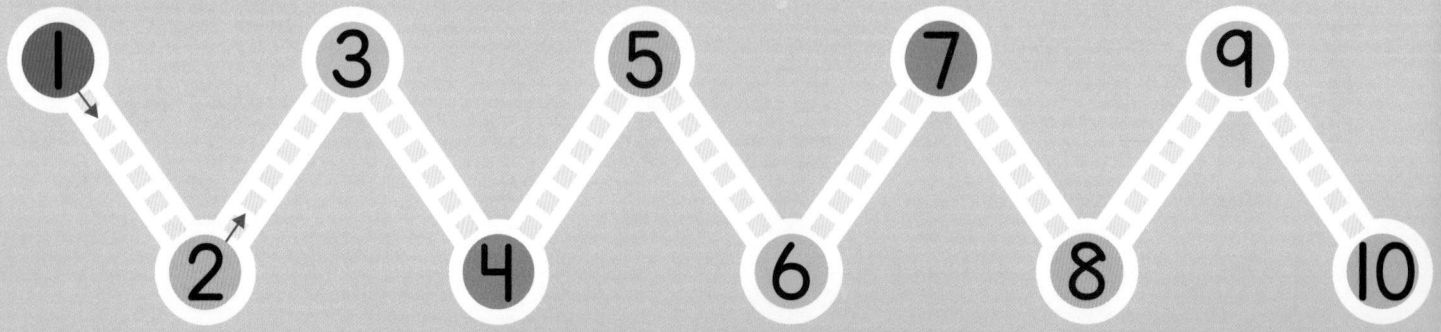

Draw a line from 1 to 5.

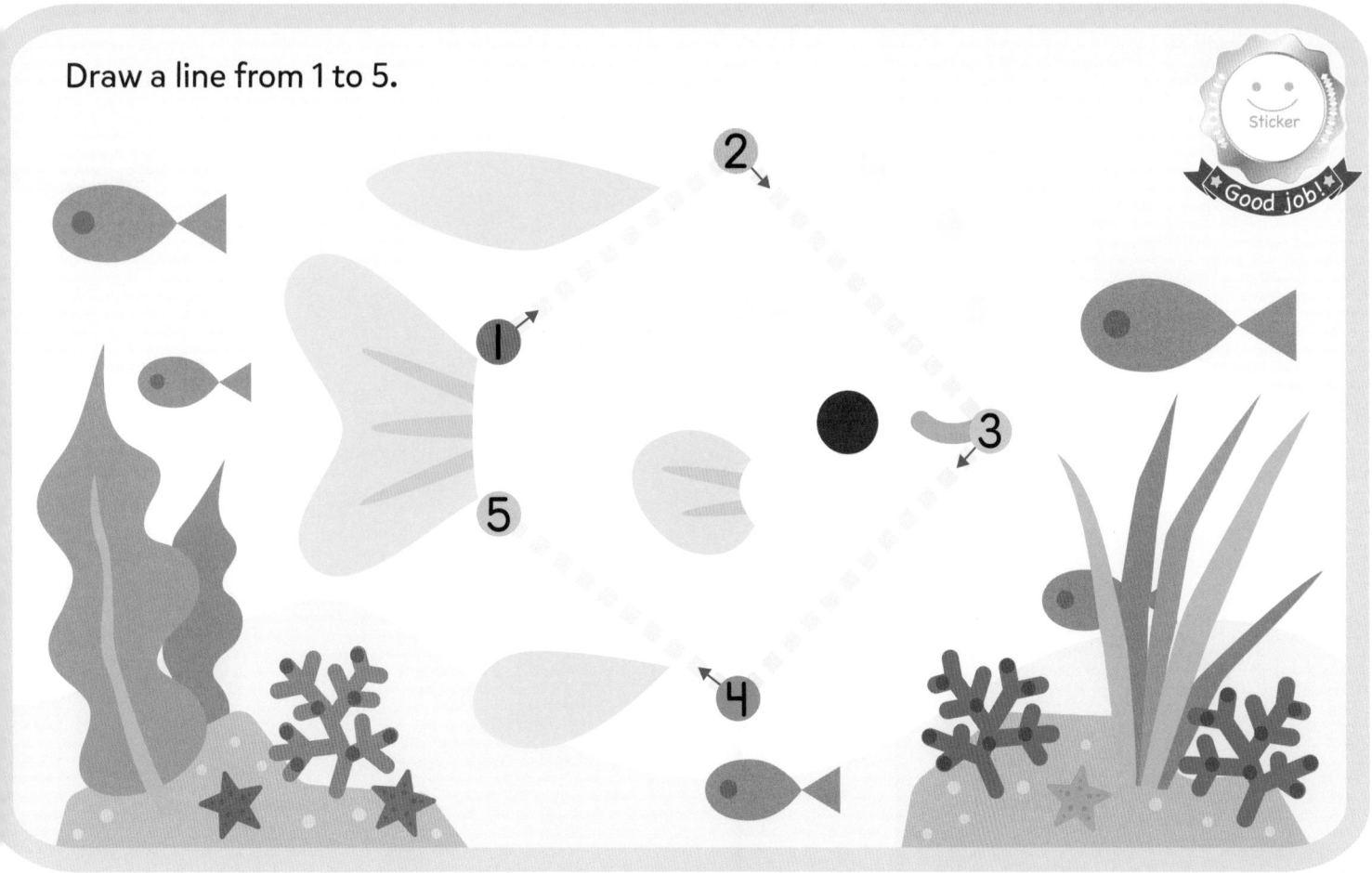

Draw a line from 1 to 10.

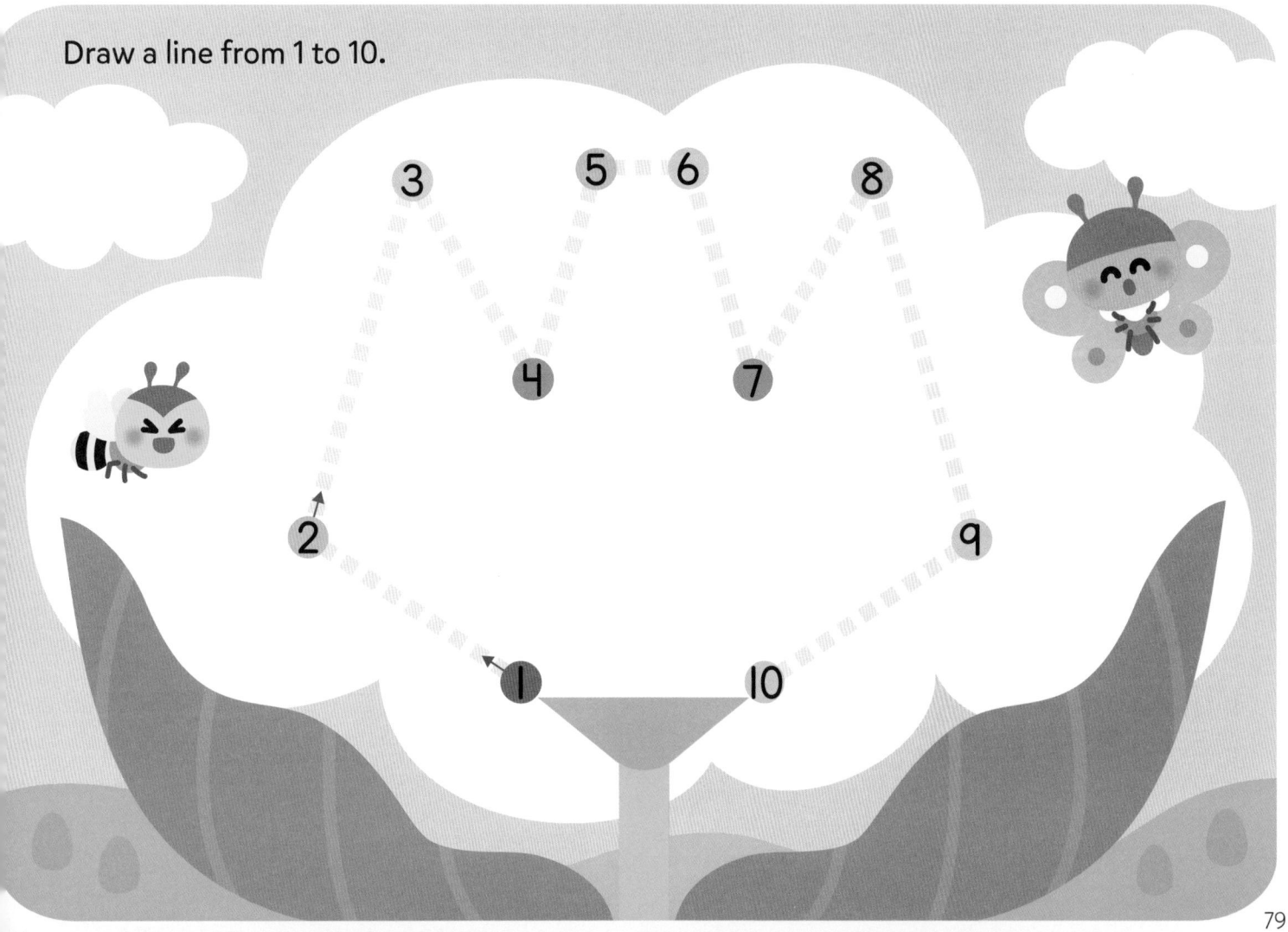

Shapes Trace the shapes.

circle

square

triangle

rectangle

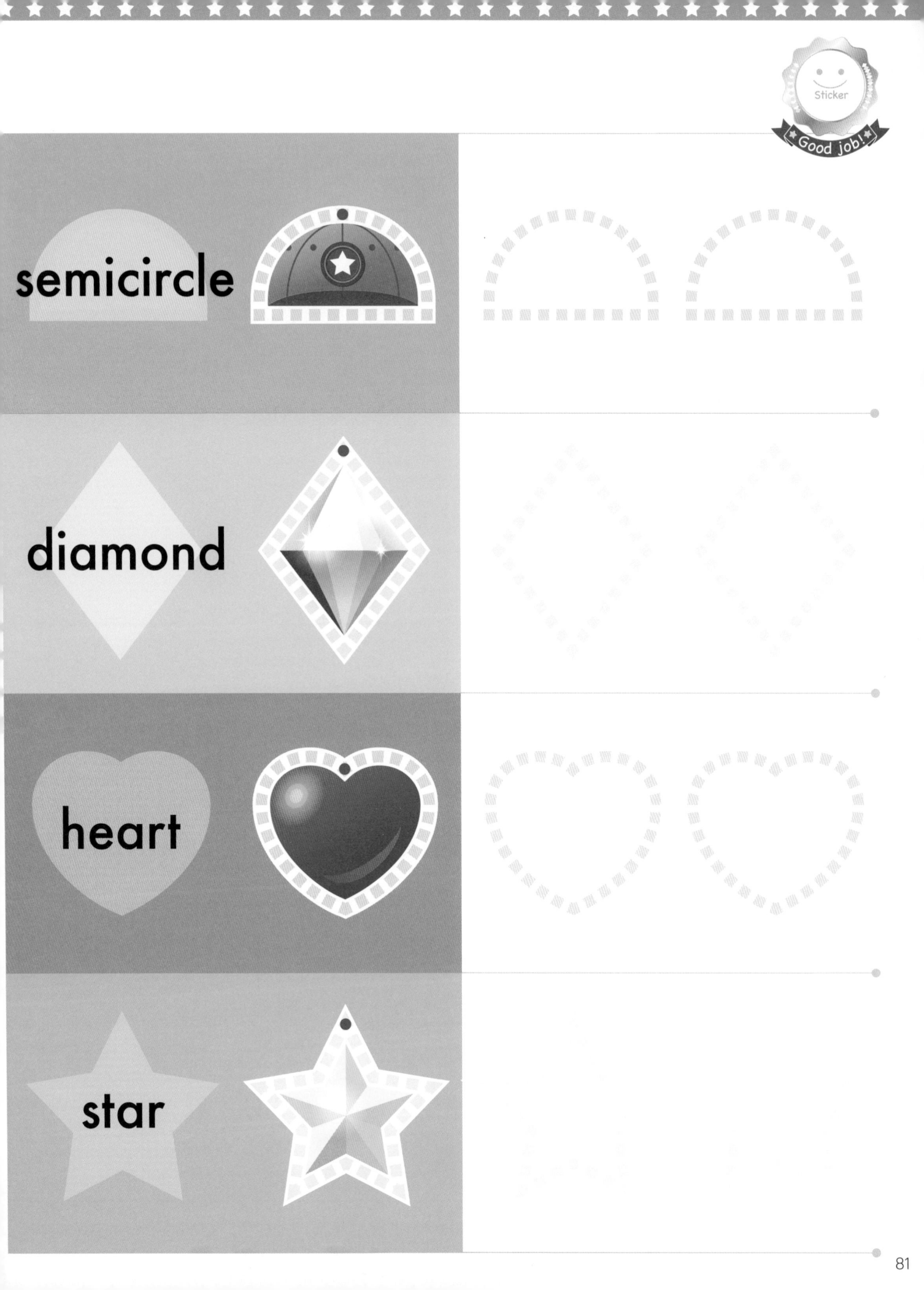
Sticker
Good job!
semicircle
diamond
heart
star

Practice writing your name and age.

Sticker

Good job

First, write your child's name. Then, have your child try to write it.

My name is...

First, write your child's age. Then, have your child try to write it.

I am...

years old.

ALPHABET

Remove this page from the book and tack it on a wall.

NUMBERS

Remove this page from the book and tack it on a wall.

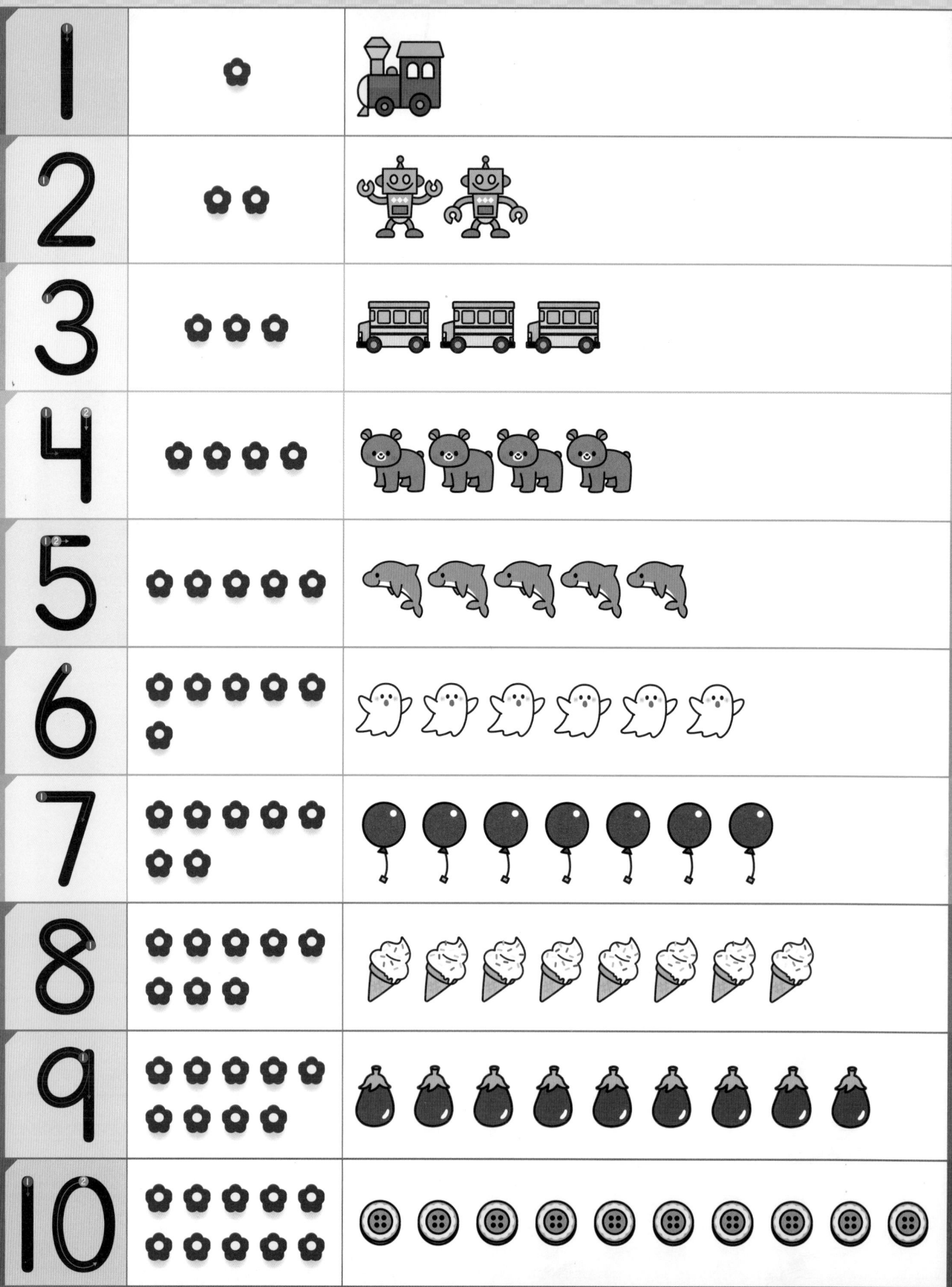